MANAGING QUALITY
AND STANDARDS

**Managing Universities and Colleges:
Guides to Good Practice**

Series editors:

David Warner, Principal and Chief Executive, Swansea
Institute of Higher Education

David Palfreyman, Bursar and Fellow, New College, Oxford

This series has been commissioned in order to provide reference
manuals of good practice on the major areas of the management of
colleges and universities.

Current titles
John M. Gledhill: *Managing Students*
Colleen Liston: *Managing Quality and Standards*

Forthcoming titles include
Judith Elkin and Derek Law (eds): *Managing Information*
Christine Humfrey: *Managing International Students*
David Watson: *Managing Strategy*

MANAGING QUALITY
AND STANDARDS

Colleen Liston

Open University Press
Buckingham · Philadelphia

Open University Press
Celtic Court
22 Ballmoor
Buckingham
MK18 1XW

email: enquiries@openup.co.uk
world wide web: http://www.openup.co.uk

and

325 Chestnut Street
Philadelphia, PA 19106, USA

First Published 1999

A catalogue record of this book is available from the British Library

ISBN   0 335 20208 X (pb)   0 335 20209 8 (hb)

Library of Congress Cataloging-in-Publication Data
Liston, Colleen, 1943–
    Managing quality and standards / Colleen Liston.
        p.   cm. – (Managing colleges and universities)
    Includes bibliographical references and index.
    ISBN 0-335-20209-8 (hardcover). – ISBN 0-335-20208-X (pbk.)
    1. Education, Higher–Great Britain–Administration.
2. Education, Higher–Standards–Great Britain.   3. Total quality
management–Great Britain.   I. Title.   II. Series.
LB2341.8.G7L57   1999
378.1'01'0941–dc21   98-29065
                                                                 CIP

Typeset by Graphicraft Limited, Hong Kong
Printed in Great Britain by St Edmundsbury Press Limited,
Bury St Edmunds, Suffolk

CONTENTS

Series editors' introduction   ix
List of figures and tables   xii
Preface   xiii
Acknowledgements   xvi

1   Introduction: terms, principles and practices   **1**

       Definition of terms   1
       Principles and practices   4

2   Historical aspects of the quality debate   **8**

       Can quality be defined?   8
         Historical overview   8
         The role of the Japanese   9
         The US experience   10
         Quality as service: applicability to the
           public sector   10
         Defining quality   11
         W. Edwards Deming   17
       Application to post-secondary education   18
       Myths and caveats   20

**3   Quality assurance in post-secondary education:
       an international overview**   **22**

       Introduction   22
       Accreditation and quality audit   22

Beliefs about accreditation 24
Problems for accreditation 25
Why conduct accreditation? 26
Accountability 26
Standards 27
How standards are set 28
Caveats on setting standards 29
Competency-based standards 30
Objectives and standards 31
The use of standards 32
Linking standards and education 33
'Graduateness' 35
Terminology 36
Licensure 36
Certification 37
Credentialing 37
Outcomes in accreditation 37
Common elements in accreditation models 39
Summarizing accreditation 41
International overview of quality assurance
methods and agencies 42
Born in the USA 42
The UK experience 43
And in Australia 44
South Africa takes up the challenge 45
Whither Canada? 46
China 47
Hong Kong 47
Europe spreads a net 47
The Netherlands moves internationally 48
New Zealand moves to the next phase 49
Why? What next? Who are the beneficiaries? 49

4   **Quality improvement in education
environments**   **51**

Introduction 51
Principles 51
Processes 53
Programme and planning reviews 53
A model for programme and planning review 56
A model for course reviews 59
Tools 66

Measurement   67
Evaluation   68
  Historical overview   68
  Uses of evaluation   70
Costs and casualties   71

5   Linking quality management to planning   `74`

Introduction   74
Setting strategic directions   74
  A framework for strategic initiatives   75
  Key questions to ask in setting directions   76
  Scenario planning   76
  Deciding on the optimum structure   77
Strategy setting in planning   78
  Workforce planning   78
  Personnel management   79
  Components of personnel management   81
  Checklist for staff development planning   84
  Performance management   86
Use of indicators   88
  The purpose of indicators   89
  Quantitative and qualitative indicators   89
  Limitations on use of indicators   90
Focusing on outcomes   95

6   Benchmarking and best practice   `98`

Introduction   98
Benchmarking: a tool or a process?   98
  Typology of benchmarking   99
  Benefits of benchmarking   100
What is best practice?   100
Rationale and guidelines for achieving best practice   102
  Best practice key point 1: Leadership   102
  Best practice key point 2: Strategy, policy and
    planning   103
  Best practice key point 3: Information and
    analysis   105
  Best practice key point 4: People   106
  Best practice key point 5: Client focus   108
  Best practice key point 6: Quality of process,
    product and service   109

Best practice key point 7: Organizational
performance 110
Example of a best practice checklist (research) 111
Postgraduate training best practice checklist 113
Best practice in teaching 115
Feedback on client satisfaction and best practice 116
Assessing the attributes of graduates to confirm
best practice 117
Competitiveness 119

7 Models to consider 121

Introduction 121
Total quality management 121
Service success models 124
The total quality service model 124
The role of the leader in service success 126
Five phases in service success 128
Client service best practice checklist 129
ISO 9000 standards 131
Origins of ISO standards 131
ISO 9000 standards clauses for education 132
Applicability to post-secondary education 133
Key points in adopting an ISO 9000 standards
approach 135
Relationships between ISO 9000 standards and
other quality frameworks 137
ISO 9000: conclusion 139
Cycle time reduction (CTR) 140
Quality awards criteria 143

8 Pulling the threads together 145

Introduction 145
Future directions 145
Whither diversity? 151
The last word on managing 152

Appendix: Definition of terms 156

Notes 161
Bibliography 180
Index 186

SERIES EDITORS'
INTRODUCTION

Post-secondary educational institutions can be viewed from a variety of different perspectives. For the majority of students and staff who work in them, they are centres of learning and teaching where the participants are there by choice and consequently, by and large, work very hard. Research has always been important in some higher education institutions, but in recent years this emphasis has grown and what for many was a great pleasure and, indeed, a treat is becoming more of a threat and an insatiable performance indicator which just has to be met. Maintaining the correct balance between quality research and learning/teaching, while the unit of resource continues to decline inexorably, is one of the key issues facing us all. Educational institutions as workplaces must be positive and not negative environments.

From another aspect, post-secondary educational institutions are clearly communities, functioning to all intents and purposes like small towns and internally requiring and providing a similar range of services, while also having very specialist needs. From yet another, they are seen as external suppliers of services to industry, commerce and the professions. These 'customers' receive, *inter alia*, a continuing flow of well qualified fresh graduates with transferable skills, part-time and short course study opportunities through which to develop existing employees, consultancy services to solve problems and help to expand business, and research and development support to create new breakthroughs.

However, educational institutions are also significant businesses in their own right. One recent study of the economic impact of higher education in Wales shows that it is of similar importance in employment terms to the steel or banking/finance sectors. Put another way,

Welsh higher education institutions (HEIs) spend half a billion pounds annually and create more than 23,000 full-time equivalent jobs. And it must be remembered that there are only 13 HEIs in Wales, compared with 175 in the whole of the UK, and that these Welsh institutions are, on average, relatively small. In addition, it has recently been realized that UK higher education is a major export industry with the added benefit of long-term financial and political returns. If the UK further education sector is also added to this equation, then the economic impact of post-secondary education is of truly startling proportions.

Whatever perspective you take, it is obvious that educational institutions require managing and, consequently, this series has been produced to facilitate that end. The editors have striven to identify authors who are distinguished practitioners in their own right and can also write. The authors have been given the challenge of producing essentially practical handbooks which combine appropriate theory and contextual material with many examples of good practice and guidance.

The topics chosen are of key importance to educational management and stand at the forefront of current debate. Some of these topics have never been covered in depth before, and all of them are equally applicable to further as well as higher education. The editors are firmly of the belief that the UK distinction between these sectors will continue to blur and will be replaced, as in many other countries, by a continuum where the management issues are entirely common.

For well over a decade, both of the editors have been involved with a management development programme for senior staff from higher education institutions throughout the world. Every year the participants quickly learn that we share the same problems and that similar solutions are normally applicable. Political and cultural differences may on occasion be important, but are often no more than an overlying veneer. Hence, this series will be of considerable relevance and value to post-secondary educational managers in many countries.

It is, therefore, very refreshing that this launch volume in the series should be written by an Australian author who has taken great pains to take the educational quality and standards debate out of its normal country-specific context. In addition, Professor Liston provides an invaluable historical dimension for the debate, tracing its origins in manufacturing industry and showing how the principles and practices involved have been adapted and modified by the educational sector. The editors, however, are particularly pleased with the numerous checklists and action plans which this book contains.

It is not only a comprehensive study of the topic, but also a book which will naturally 'fall open' at various points throughout the text because of heavy and continuous use as a reference document.

David Warner
David Palfreyman

LIST OF FIGURES
AND TABLES

Figure 2.1	Quality management with a client focus	20
Figure 4.1	Sample of an education institution quality cycle	54
Figure 4.2	Example of a cycle for planning and review	55
Figure 4.3	Flowchart of programme and planning review	60
Figure 5.1	Links between workforce planning, personnel management, training and development, and corporate strategic planning	81
Figure 5.2	Links between workforce planning, personnel management, training and development, and corporate/division/area strategic planning	82
Figure 5.3	Influences on post-secondary education objectives	91
Figure 5.4	Major sources of influence on the post-secondary education sector	91
Figure 5.5	Key elements in a quality system	96
Figure 6.1	Examples of benchmarking performance	101
Figure 7.1	Quality service paradigm contingency model	125
Figure 7.2	Areas of application of the ISO 9000 standards clauses in education	134
Figure 8.1	The changing quality paradigm	149
Table 2.1	Quality management principles of five quality gurus	12–16
Table 5.1	Workforce planning links	80

PREFACE

In writing a book on managing quality and standards in the post-secondary education sector, it is acknowledged at the outset that the topic creates images of *quality police* and extra work. Dispelling fear and discomfort is one of the key objectives of the book, and another is increasing knowledge and understanding of the practice.

The expectations of readers have been anticipated. The text is structured as eight chapters which may be read straight through or individually. A comprehensive summary of terms defined stipulatively in most cases, or in a manner that will be useful for interpreting the text, can be found in the Appendix. Definitions of immediate importance are presented in Chapter 1 to set the scene for interpretations made by the author.

One of the problems associated with the quality debate, and to a lesser extent with the notion of standards in relation to performance measurement and *best practice*, is the use of language and jargon. Identification of how terms are interpreted and used throughout will provide clarity for the reader.

A number of suggestions are made on how to incorporate principles of quality management and use of standards into systems and day-to-day operations. Rather than being an *add-on* as a necessity for external accountability, the value of a quality approach will be conveyed through the presentation of frameworks and guidelines for immediate use. A number of subheadings are included in each chapter as *signposts* to important principles, guidelines, tools and checklists that can be applied in practice.

Chapter 1 defines key terms, provides a brief overview of principles and practices for managing quality in post-secondary education and introduces the international perspective. The concept of quality may vary among people and nations, but there is evidence of greater awareness of its importance in the global market place.

To convey understanding of the origins of the quality movement, Chapter 2 explores the history of quality management (which began in the manufacturing sector) and relates the concept of quality to the post-secondary education sector. The vexed issue of linking quality and standards to accreditation of institutions or to the *graduateness* of those who undertake educational programmes is addressed in Chapter 3.

Models of quality assurance audits and accreditation are presented to provide an international overview of practice. Illumination of similarities between the systems and mechanisms used, and the experimentation with new models for sometimes dubious reasons (often politically based), is intended to provide a catalyst for sector-wide cooperation and coordination to take back control of managing quality in post-secondary education. The instability created by changing governments and political whims provides a heavy burden on the sector and fosters cynicism and frustration, particularly among academics. Background information on standards setting, and the criteria for licensure and registration of graduates, is included.

Chapter 4 is a source of principles for quality systems; guidelines for quality improvement practices; examples of review processes; information on quality tools; discussion of measurement methods and evaluation; and considers the costs and casualties of some quality management models. The chapter can be used by those involved in quality improvement and advancement in their institution as well as by managers and general and academic staff in their own activities.

Of critical importance is the interrelationship between planning and quality management. In Chapter 5, linking mechanisms are explored through an example of workforce planning. Advice on direction setting and important questions to be addressed are included at the beginning of the chapter to provide guidelines to those involved in planning and quality management. Scenario planning is explained, and the strengths and weaknesses of various hierarchical structures are presented.

The topic of performance management is introduced to emphasize the further important link between planning, quality management and staff development. The use of indicators as signposts to information that is required and to selection of measures is included. A brief overview of quantitative and qualitative criteria with guidelines for areas in which they should be developed in each operational unit is provided as a checklist.

There is a good deal of rhetoric about, and some evidence of involvement in, benchmarking in the post-secondary education sector. Common types are described in Chapter 6 and benefits suggested. The principles of *best practice* are listed and a rationale is proposed. In addition, a comprehensive framework of criteria which can be used to build best practice principles into all operations and activities is presented. The critical elements of a quality system are outlined as they relate to increased competitiveness.

Chapter 7 will be of interest to readers who wish to know more about models of quality management, including total quality management (TQM), service quality, ISO 9000 standards and process re-engineering (the example is cycle time reduction). The commonly used criteria in a range of quality awards presented to organizations around the world, which are considered to be best practice examples of quality management, are related to managing practices in the post-secondary education sector.

The purpose in Chapter 8 is to pull together the threads in the book to provide a fabric for the future. What the future holds for the diverse nature of post-secondary education institutions and their offerings is considered. Finally, placing the quality management debate in the context of management theory provides a mechanism to highlight the benefits of incorporating quality improvement into every activity: that is, transforming the quality management paradigm in post-secondary education from one of accountability (to external agents) to improvement (for the good of all associated with each institution).

ACKNOWLEDGEMENTS

Without the support and assistance of several people this book would not have been written. First, I am grateful for the confidence of colleagues in quality management in recommending me to Professor David Warner, who commissioned the book as one in a series, and for their feedback on my writing. In particular I acknowledge the invaluable assistance and generosity of Professor David Witmer in Wisconsin, who critically reviewed my work and provided, with Doris, a congenial haven and home away from home.

Second, I thank the management at Curtin University of Technology for granting me study leave and supporting my quality office staff, especially Catherine, in carrying on in my absence. Third, I express my heartfelt thanks to Christine, Matthew, Marco, Michelle and Marcus for technical assistance and advice on computing and diagrams. They are my friends as well as my capable and committed staff.

It is not possible to acknowledge adequately the sacrifices made by my husband Richard, who took leave from his own job to act as porter, computer technician, chauffeur, proof reader, editor, typist and amateur psychologist in times of stress! None the less, I dedicate this book to him in the hope that working with me on it will enrich his own workplace.

1

INTRODUCTION: TERMS, PRINCIPLES AND PRACTICES

Is *quality* a state of mind? Perhaps an attitude prompted by a name or brand? In an era of unclear boundaries and inconsistencies in policies and procedures, it has become important for post-secondary education institutions to develop clear missions and goals within their own values frameworks to present themselves in the global market place. One of the ways of communicating the unique or highly credible nature of a particular institution and its programmes is to describe its *quality*.

Attention to quality and standards in post-secondary education institutions, whose boundaries are merging across the sector and within the sector, is increasing. Since the early 1990s there have been a number of international conferences and symposia on the topic. Texts and journals have been produced at an ever-increasing rate around the globe, and governments of all persuasions are more and more interested in quality – especially as a means to address accountability and funding. In order to understand the magnitude or scope of the quality, some sort of measure or level or *standard* is required to enable the potential user or consumer to form an opinion on the offering. Standards are therefore becoming an issue in the education (especially the post-secondary) sector, and rapidly these will be established globally. This is already the case in the profession of engineering, and moves are evident in other areas.

Definition of terms

A selection of terms and definitions from the Appendix is included here. They are chosen for their role in prevailing language and jargon in quality management, and to set the scene for how the words and concepts are used in the book.

Benchmarking

A tool used to improve products, services or management processes by analysing the best practices of other companies or institutions (organizations) to determine standards or performance, and how to achieve them in order to increase customer (client, stakeholder) satisfaction.

Best practice

The best way to do something. The concept can be applied at all levels of the organization, from the total management system down to individual functions. It is a changing concept as improved processes are integrated into the organization.

Clients

All those with a legitimate interest in the training system or individual training organizations. They include:

- customers (e.g. learners and enterprises);
- owners (e.g. governments and ministries, shareholders);
- fund providers and agencies (e.g. government departments of education and private training investors);
- staff;
- sub-suppliers (e.g. child care centre contractors, business and industry for specialist lectures);
- regulatory bodies (e.g. training or regulatory boards with legislative requirements, accreditation councils and agencies);
- stakeholders (e.g. industry, professional associations, advocacy groups);
- the community.

The term *client* is often despised in the education sector (along with other jargon), but is used to encompass not only students but also stakeholders such as private and public owners and funding agencies, professions and industry, potential employers and graduates with future needs for lifelong learning through continuing education. *Client*, rather than *customer*, is the term selected for use in this text on managing quality and standards in post-secondary education.

Customers

The individuals or groups who directly use the products or services of any organization. Customers can be external or internal. For education providers, the external customers are principally learners and professional organizations or business enterprises. Internal customers are those who receive products (e.g. information, courses, research findings) and services (e.g. teaching, instruction, research supervision, consultancy) from other parts of the education or training system or those who share internal work relationships within the organization. It is not essential that any payment be made for a product or service for a recipient to be designated as a customer.

Some organizations use the words *client* and *customer* interchangeably, while others differentiate clients as those who pay for a service or product, or who receive a professional service.

International standards (ISO 9000)

Describe the elements that quality systems should encompass but not how these elements should be designed or implemented. They will be influenced by the particular objectives, products, processes and individual practices of an organization.

Mission

The core reason for being of an organization. Best expressed in the form of a statement no longer than 25 to 50 words.

Performance indicators

Indicators used by operational units, schools and departments to demonstrate the extent to which programmes are achieving the desired results. The three dimensions of programme performance (appropriateness, efficiency, effectiveness) should be considered in context.

Process

A particular method of doing something, generally involving a number of steps or operations. The organization of people, equipment, energy, procedures and material into the work activities needed to produce a specified end result (work product). A sequence of repeatable interrelated activities characterized as having specific, measurable inputs, value-added activities and specific, measurable outputs.

Quality

The total effect of the features of a process, product or service on its performance, or on the customer's or client's perception of that performance. It is not just a feature of a finished product or service but involves a focus on internal processes and outputs and includes the reduction of waste and the improvement of productivity. In post-secondary education one single definition is problematic. Quality is related more to the relevance and value of each institution's mission, purpose, goals and objectives, and the achievement of identified outcomes.

Principles and practices

The key elements of any quality system must be designed in consideration of the needs of its clients. Standards or principles reflecting clients' needs and incorporating current understandings of knowledge and best practice should be established. A self-assessment and meta-evaluation process provides a means of comprehensively determining whether management procedures, courses and support services are meeting the standards or principles.

An independent appraisal of the self-assessment by external validators can provide evidence for those wishing to assess accountability for both quality review and funding purposes. The role of performance indicators and the relationship between efficiency and effectiveness in judging performance is discussed in Chapter 5. The relevance of indicators and their value for providing information about quality can be judged as part of the external assessment process, which is conducted by external quality assurance organizations such as government quality auditors and funding bodies, or accreditation agencies on behalf of professions or others.

The global business and professional market place seeks personnel with wide-ranging educational and training backgrounds. Human resource departments are looking for ways to evaluate courses and degrees equitably, not only from within their own countries but from others around the world. There are two current players in the transnational standards field. One is the ISO 9000 series of auditable quality standards and the other is the evolving Global Alliance for Transnational Education (GATE). The former is a system developed by the International Organisation for Standardisation, which was founded in 1947 and is a federation of about 120 nations. The latter was founded in the USA in 1995 and has affiliates in South Africa, Canada, Chile, Mexico, Ireland, China, New Zealand, Australia and the UK. The United Nations Education, Scientific and Cultural Organisation (UNESCO), the Organisation for Economic Cooperation and Development (OECD) and the International Network of Quality Assurance Agencies in Higher Education (INQAAHE) are also founding affiliates.

Affiliates and staff of the Center for Quality Assurance in International Education and GATE have proposed a set of Principles for Transnational Education Courses (Degree Programmes). The Principles provide a basis for reviewing courses offered internationally. They are broad-ranging and address the following eight elements:

1 *Goals and objectives*. Participants who enrol should understand the goals and objectives which fit appropriately in the provider's purposes and competencies.
2 *Standards*. The provider must ensure that courses are comparable with, and meet the educational quality criteria of, those offered by the provider in its own country.
3 *Legal matters*. Transnational courses and programmes must comply with all appropriate laws of the host country.
4 *Student enrolment and admission*. Participants must be treated equitably and ethically. Full disclosure of pertinent information and full student status or equivalent with the provider organisation must pertain.
5 *Human resources*. There must be a sufficient number of fully qualified persons to provide courses and programmes. Activities must be supervised and regularly evaluated by the provider.
6 *Physical and financial resources*. The provider must assure that an adequate learning environment and sufficient appropriate resources are available until all obligations to enrolled participants are fulfilled.
7 *Teaching and learning*. Courses and programmes must be pedagogically sound with respect to the methods of provision and the nature and needs of the participants.
8 *Evaluation*. Courses and programmes must be regularly and appropriately evaluated as a normal part of the provider organization's activities, with the results of the evaluations used for improvement.

A range of criteria for each principle clarifies requirements subject to external review. The principles were developed by GATE, which has identified its role in three areas of need:

1 A reliable and current database of transnational educational programmes globally.
2 Cooperatively to develop principles of good practice.

3 An international forum to coordinate quality assurance and other activities related to principled advocacy of transnational programmes.[1]

The inevitable globalization of the post-secondary educational market place and a world market for international students, estimated by UNESCO back in 1992 to be more than 1.2 million, has moved the need for international and transnational standards into sharper focus. The exact number of participants in courses taken in their own country from an international source is unknown. Countries enrolling students from other countries count them, but numbers are unknown for those enrolled for corporate and international courses.

Economic growth is dictating much of the change in the nature of the delivery of education. As importers, the USA, Canada, the UK, France and Germany are high on the list. The principal exporters are the USA, the UK and Australia. Earnings for the USA in 1994 were around US$7 billion and in Australia for 1993 around US$1 billion. In 1997, the estimate for Australia rose to around US$2 billion. Along with the exponential growth in development of new technologies to enhance delivery, making distance education an easy alternative, there is recognition of the transnational education market place.

Human capital (and post-secondary education, especially the higher education sector, is part of the human capital development sector) is critical for the future wealth, health and survival of the planet. Education enrolment rates in developing nations are rising. Since the 1960s there has been a 25 per cent rise in participation rates to 95 per cent of the expected age cohort for East Asians. Expenditure on primary level education is rising at a remarkable rate compared with growth in national economy in countries such as Korea, Mexico and some in Africa.[2]

As Richard Lewis, Pro-Vice-Chancellor of the Open University (UK), points out when discussing the term *graduate*, the nature of qualifications and degree equivalence: 'These issues are important, particularly from the point of view of students who need to know how their qualifications will rate in the world scales and, having invested their time and money, need to know that their qualifications have maximum applicability across the world.'[3] He notes that professions, such as engineering, have seen the need to consider international accreditation. In 1989 the engineering accreditation bodies in Australia, Canada, Ireland, New Zealand, the UK and the USA agreed to recognize the equivalence or comparability of their accreditation processes in the *Washington Accord*.

Furthermore, the General Agreement on Trade in Services (GATS) of the World Trade Organization has encouraged the development of common standards for education, to foster mutual recognition for professionals, and to free up the processes involved in registration and licensing. There is a need to retain diversity while protecting educational quality. To this end, cooperation and partnerships between quality assurance and accreditation bodies around the world will be required. Both government and private agencies must ensure that the rigorous standards applied by some must not be compromised by deals with those prepared to sail close to the wind in the global mobility current, where quality assurance mechanisms and systems may be questionable in some countries.[4]

What is the answer? The ISO 9000 standards have been adapted to the education sector, but may not be applicable beyond the basic processes around a course or programme (unless it is competency-based). The principles espoused by GATE are very broad and do not address important issues in the area of outcomes, but they provide a basic standards framework and enough autonomy and self-regulation for education institutions. They are meant for transnational education courses.[5] What then of graduates from local courses or courses in countries other than where they intend to practise their trade or profession?[6] The vexed issue of accreditation of courses and recognition of individuals to practise is of interest to the debate and is considered in Chapter 3. In Chapter 2, the application of principles of quality management to the post-secondary education sector, based on a historical perspective, is presented.

2
HISTORICAL ASPECTS OF THE QUALITY DEBATE

Can quality be defined?

A glossary of terms has been provided in Chapter 1. Has this clarified the meaning of the word *quality*? Quality may be understood as a concept, but there are many definitions of quality. Some historical points of note provide a background to the concept of quality management, and demonstrate why definitions of quality vary contextually.

Historical overview

There is no intention to provide a comprehensive historical review here, but the background is important to an understanding of concepts of quality management in post-secondary education. A brief overview, highlighting the major steps, including the significant involvement of Japanese proponents of the quality movement and W. Edwards Deming, is presented for those who are interested in the fascinating journey.

The quality movement began in the early 1900s when a British farmer, Ronald A. Fisher, devised a way of organizing a series of crop growing experiments (with a few test runs) to determine cause and effect relationships. In the 1930s, Walter A. Shewhart of Bell Laboratories used statistical process control (SPC) to study variation in the performance of systems.[1] W. Edwards Deming, a statistician and a student of Shewhart, helped engineers and operators in the war years to accomplish tasks such as the production of bullets. His efforts were not appreciated in his home country, the USA, but he and his ideas were embraced by the Japanese.

Following the war years, interest in the use of SPC decreased. Deming focused on his theory of management based on quality principles, i.e. management responsibility for quality rather than a focus on technical aspects. The quality approach then took hold in Japan, with the Japanese Union of Scientists and Engineers (JUSE) using the services of Juran, Armand and Feigenbaum – consultants on quality. Deming's contribution was recognized by the establishment of the Deming Prize by JUSE in 1951. In 1981, when Deming had reached the age of 81 years, his work was finally recognized in North America, where quality was largely ignored until the 1970s. Deming died in 1993. Interestingly, quality management was not taught in schools or universities in the Western world until the early 1990s, and only then in pioneering institutions.[2]

The role of the Japanese

The Japanese involvement in the history of the quality movement is particularly interesting. Kaoru Ishikawa was championing total quality control before the Second World War and, among others, created the concept of *quality circles*. He was a professor at the University of Tokyo and a founder of JUSE.[3] Genichi Taguchi proposed that loss resulted from what he termed *non-quality*, and suggested that quality and reliability had to be built in at the design stage. He was one of the first people to advocate prototyping (known as the Taguchi method), and won the Deming Prize four times.[4]

The concept of *zero defects*, immortalized by Crosby many years later, was developed by Shigeo Shingo. He believed that processes should become mistake-proof by design and control, or *poka-yoke*, e.g. designing a headlight so that it can only be installed the right way up.[5] Imai later extended the concept of zero defects using a continuous improvement process termed *kaizen*, which is a never ending search for ever higher levels of quality by identifying the causes of defects.[6]

In Japan, quality control is everyone's responsibility and not just assigned to the quality control experts. The culture is one of worker empowerment and long-term investment in the training and competence of front-line workers.[7] It is acknowledged that stakeholders in quality are not just the external customers and clients or the major investors in a company, but also fellow workers who depend on the quality of others' work. Measurement has to be very accurate, so that even the most minute errors can be detected and rectified to avoid ultimate quality defects.[8] The success of Japanese manufacturers since the 1960s can be related to this management philosophy.

The US experience

During the 1970s, manufacturers in the USA began to regret their lack of focus on building quality into production processes. It was becoming uncomfortably evident that the Japanese were winning more of a share of the market. In response, organizations in the USA developed a more formal approach to specifying, documenting and measuring quality requirements.

In the late 1970s, Philip B. Crosby began to expound the advantages of a quality approach to management based on the Japanese success and his 14 years of personal experience as a corporate vice president for quality. He pulled together the American and Japanese quality thinking, bringing to it pragmatic realism, and expounded five key elements necessary for quality management:

1 Whatever is produced should conform to requirements rather than specifications.
2 Quality must be measured by the cost of not conforming to requirements.
3 Quality is not a choice based on economic factors; it is essential for survival.
4 Management should be satisfied with nothing less than zero defects, for which it has responsibility and which cannot be seen as a worker problem.
5 Problems originate throughout the organization and must be attributed to specific areas of origin by management to rectify those problems.[9]

Thus *quality assurance* became the term for attempting to improve quality by developing selected quality control techniques within a management framework. The emphasis was on preventing rather than curing errors.[10]

Quality as service: applicability to the public sector

By the mid-1990s the first wave of quality reform, characterized by industrially constructed total quality management (TQM) principles (which are presented in Chapter 7) and a statistical focus for standards and production control, had given way to a second wave focusing on meeting customer needs and value creation. This fusion of quality and service concepts, drawn from the business world and adapted to meet the specific environment of education institutions, is likely to drive reform into the next century. There is also likely to be increasing globalization of reform efforts using benchmarking and best practice principles. Experimentation with this emerging management philosophy in the public sector during the 1980s has been captured and, in varying degrees, explained by a number of authors.[11] It is being translated for application to the post-secondary education sector. More generally, the concept of a socially constructed quality management paradigm that is tailored to service organizations, can be found in the work of Karl Albrecht.[12]

A summary of the key principles and philosophies of a number of these gurus of the quality movement can be found in Table 2.1.

Defining quality

Quality is related to a body of knowledge about products, services and customer and client satisfaction. The term is not a synonym for *excellence* or *goodness*. Like the word *run*, quality has many meanings. Quality does not mean *up-market* (e.g. quality car, quality food), so perspective is important. Definitions of quality include:

- fitness for use (Juran);
- conformance to requirements (Crosby);
- product or service which helps someone and enjoys good sustainable markets (Deming);
- provision to internal and external customers of innovative products and services which fully satisfy their needs (Xerox);
- what your customer perceives it to be, i.e. consistently meeting customers' needs and expectations and developing the full potential of the resources used in the process (Feigenbaum).

How can these early definitions be summarized to describe the key elements in approaching quality? A *quality approach* focuses on:

- identifying and satisfying client needs;
- developing and tapping the full potential of staff;
- improving key processes.

As such, the approach provides a way of running an organization. The main themes and principles are:

1 Led from the top.
2 Client-focused.
3 Involves everyone (or seeks to) and develops potential.
4 Process-oriented (linking cause and effect).

Table 2.1 Quality management principles of five quality gurus

Deming's 14 points	Juran's ten steps	Feigenbaum's ten benchmarks	Crosby's 14 steps	Peters's 12 attributes
Create constancy of purpose to improve product and service	*Build awareness* of the need and the opportunity for improvement	Quality is *a companywide process*	Make it clear that *management is committed to quality*	*Management obsession with quality* – practical action backed up by emotional commitment
Adopt new philosophy for new economic age by management learning responsibilities and taking leadership for change	*Set goals* for improvement	Quality is *what the customer says it is*	Form *quality improvement teams* with senior representatives from each department	*Passionate systems* – failure will occur if there is a system without passion or vice versa, and an ideology is important, though not one necessarily based on a particular guru
Cease dependence on inspection to achieve quality; eliminate the need for mass inspection by building quality into the product	*Organize to reach the goals* (establish a quality council, identify problems, select projects, appoint teams, designate facilitators)	*Quality and cost are a sum, not a difference*	*Measure* processes to determine where current and potential quality problems lie	*Measurement of quality* – this should be a feature from the start, enacted by everybody, and the results of it widely displayed

End awarding business on price, instead minimize total cost and move towards single suppliers for items	*Provide training*	Quality requires both *individual and team zealots*	Evaluate the cost of *quality* and explain its use as a management tool	*Quality is rewarded* – recognizing quality achievement with tangible rewards provides the incentive to bring about breakthroughs in attitude
Improve constantly and forever the system of production and service to improve quality and productivity and to decrease costs	*Carry out projects* to solve problems	Quality is *a way of managing*	Raise the *quality awareness* and personal concern of all employees	*Everyone is trained for quality* – extensive training should apply to all in the company, and this should encompass instruction in cause and effect analysis, statistical process control, and group interaction
Institute training on the job	*Report progress*	*Quality and innovation are mutually dependant*	*Take actions to correct problems* identified through previous steps	*Multi-function teams* – teams which span the traditional organizational structures should be introduced; quality circles or, to be more recommended, cross-functional teams such as error cause removal or corrective action teams

Table 2.1 (continued)

Deming's 14 points	Juran's ten steps	Feigenbaum's ten benchmarks	Crosby's 14 steps	Peters's 12 attributes
Institute leadership; supervision should be to help to do a better job; overhaul supervision of management and production workers	*Give recognition*	Quality is *an ethic*	Establish *progress monitoring* for the improvement process	*Small is beautiful* – there is significance in every change and no such thing as a small improvement
Drive out fear so that all may work effectively for the organization	*Communicate results*	Quality requires *continuous improvement*	*Train supervisors* to actively carry out their part of the quality improvement programme	*Create endless 'Hawthorne' effects* – new events are the antidote to the doldrums or flagging interest in quality
Break down barriers between departments; research, design, sales and production must work together to foresee problems in production and use	*Keep score*	Quality is *the most cost-effective, least capital-intensive route to productivity*	Hold a *zero defects day* to let everyone realize that there has been a change and to reaffirm management commitment	*Parallel organizational structure devoted to quality improvement* – this describes the creation of shadow quality teams and emphasizes that it is a route through which hourly paid workers can progress

Eliminate slogans, exhortations, and numerical targets for the workforce, such as zero defects or new productivity levels. Such exhortations are divisive, as the bulk of the problems belong to the system and are beyond the power of the workforce

Eliminate quotas or work standards, and management by objectives or numerical goals; substitute leadership

Maintain momentum by making annual improvement part of the regular systems and processes of the company

Quality is implemented with a *total system connected with customers and suppliers*

Encourage individuals to establish *improvement goals* for themselves and their groups

Encourage individuals to communicate to management the *obstacles they face* in attaining their improvement goals

Everyone is involved – the quality process is comprehensive embracing suppliers, distributors and customers

When quality goes up, costs go down – quality improvement is the primary source of cost reduction. The elementary force at work is simplification of design, process or procedures

Table 2.1 (continued)

Deming's 14 points	Juran's ten steps	Feigenbaum's ten benchmarks	Crosby's 14 steps	Peters's 12 attributes
Remove barriers that rob people of their right to pride of workmanship; hourly workers, management and engineering; eliminate annual or merit ratings and management by objective			*Recognize* and appreciate those who participate	*Quality improvement is a never ending journey* – all quality is relative, it does not stand still
Institute a vigorous education and self-improvement programme			Establish *quality councils* to communicate on a regular basis	
Put everyone in the company to work to accomplish the transformation			*Do it all over again* to emphasize that the quality improvement programme never ends	

Source: Adapted from Morgan and Murgatroyd (1994) and Albrecht (1992).

5 Prevention strategies (not the detection of errors).
6 Fosters cooperation and win–win relationships.
7 Focuses on continuous improvement (goalposts shift).
8 Aims for long-term goals.
9 Systematic and methodical approach.
10 Based on management by fact (hard data on significant issues).
11 Promotes responsibility to the public.
12 A holistic approach.

Barker, a noted futurist, predicts that quality management will be hailed as the most important paradigm shift to come out of the twentieth century.[13] Indeed, if organizations, including post-secondary education institutions, do not demonstrate its components (statistical process control, continuous improvement, benchmarking, the constant pursuit of excellence, knowing how to do the right thing the first time), not only will they not be in the game, they will not survive.

W. Edwards Deming

Deming was regarded as the *father* of the quality movement and has been elevated to god-like status by current proponents of TQM, who worship his management philosophy to the exclusion of any other management doctrines. Deming disciples have continued to multiply since his death in 1993 and, with political support at the highest levels, their influence in the US public sector is considerable. Furthermore, he is likely to remain a Japanese deity in perpetuity, through the Deming Prize. There was a distinctly religious tone that surrounded much of his work, as the following quote taken from his last book, *The New Economics*, attests:

> The first step is transformation of the individual . . . It comes from understanding of the system of profound knowledge. The individual, transformed, will perceive new meaning to his life, to events, to numbers, to interactions among people. Once the individual understands the system of profound knowledge, he will apply its principles in every kind of relationship with other people . . . The transformation will release the power of human resource contained in intrinsic motivation. In place of competition for high rating, high grades, to be Number One, there will be co-operation on problems of common interest . . . There will be joy in work, joy in learning. Anyone that enjoys his work is a pleasure to work with. Everyone will win; no losers.[14]

His *system of profound knowledge* consists of four components:

1 Appreciation for a system (describing which, he quoted from the Bible and mused about St Paul understanding a system).
2 Knowledge about variation (essentially Shewhart's work).
3 Theory of knowledge (where he postulated that without theory, experience has no meaning).
4 Psychology (understanding what is important to individuals, and in their interactions with others).

It is from a historical overview of the quality movement that the focus moves to the education sector. The principles of quality management in post-secondary education are those which apply in any organization that is considered to be *learning*.[15] Being a *learning organization* is evidenced by leadership strategies which support and encourage service quality and review, and, from a historical perspective, many of the principles are important in the TQM movement, which is presented in Chapter 7.

Application to post-secondary education

The principle of maintenance of standards is important across the education sector. Vocational and higher education is dependent on standards in secondary school sector programmes, which, in turn, rely on excellent preparatory programmes. Interactions to ensure that standards are improving rather than declining will assure the input side of Deming's model of interrelationships between input, throughput and output, which are expanded in Chapter 4. Social, political and financial pressures should not reward those who demonstrate high pass rates linked to increased attrition rates and a lowering of standards. Selection of students is a vital element underpinning improvement of the quality of both the throughput and output stages. No attempt should be made to seek less diversity in the entering cohort, but attention should be on ensuring that programmes cater for those selected and add value to their knowledge and skills. Bridging courses and other highly resource-dependent programmes to meet the needs of equity groups will continue to be important.

Economic models for the education sector see economists disagreeing and therefore, through protracted debate, having some influence on government policy in many countries. There are strengths and weaknesses in proposals which see students being able to *buy* programmes using education credit vouchers and the like, or where courses are funded privately by industry, without regard to selection on merit.[16] A mix of market forces and protection of standards can be achieved through education institutions carefully selecting students who will enhance their own knowledge and skills while advancing the outcomes for the institution.

The principles for quality in education should include: commitment to continuous improvement in teaching, research and community interactions; commitment to continuous improvement in staff and student relationships; commitment to staff development and resource management to ensure continuous improvement; commitment to evaluation and review of all activities to seek continuous improvement.

When standards and principles are developed by education institutions, they should bear in mind a range of legislative requirements (for example, in relation to equal opportunity, sexual discrimination, racial discrimination, human rights, disability discrimination and occupational health and safety), take into account the institution's own mission and values, and focus on the needs of clients. Standards should be developed across a range of functions, including: strategic management; design, development and review of courses; delivery and assessment for courses; research and consultancy; support services; human resource management; financial management and general administration (including purchasing, contractual arrangements, risk management, assets and facilities management); and organizational performance (including institutional research, quality management and audit).[17]

Figure 2.1 presents the interrelationships between standards or principles, and their attention to clients at the input, throughput and output phases. The model presented in Figure 2.1 highlights the responsibility of those in all areas to focus on clients. Everyone is responsible for the success of the organization through focusing on clients' needs. It matters little whether they are tending the grounds, building, maintaining, writing purchase orders, preparing laboratories, teaching, supervising research students, negotiating with industry, consulting with external agencies, conducting surveys, forming links with international partners, marketing or engaging in political lobbying. The clients are primarily students, but may include other internal individuals or departments, industry or business interests, professions, local and federal governments and their agencies, parents, sponsors and others who fund the institution or students, as well as those who seek partnerships and consultancy services. The clients may be locally, nationally or internationally based. Communication and relationships may be face-to-face, from a distance through mail and telephone exchanges or electronic.

Figure 2.1 Quality management with a client focus.

Underpinning any system which can provide assurances to clients about the quality of the products (e.g. courses, consultancy services, research outcomes) and services (e.g. teaching, research supervision, resource management, student support) of the education institution is improvement. The model proposed may be applied to any post-secondary organization, whether it be: (a) delivering vocational and competency-based training, or basic and higher degree courses; (b) conducting basic or applied research; (c) consulting with or serving the community. Furthermore, the model is applicable to local, international and transnational purposes.[18]

Myths and caveats

A warning is issued to beware of contracting *quality-itis*, which occurs when quality is used as an unqualified descriptor (e.g. *quality people, quality job*). Adopting a quality approach involves having a coherent set of values, policies, and mechanisms that are respected and applied throughout the organization, integrated into normal operations and applied consistently over time.[19]

A quality approach is not:

- A project or programme (e.g. audit), but an ongoing journey.
- An add-on; it is an effort to re-design and improve.
- An employee-motivation programme.
- A marketing ploy; the intention is to create new reality for clients.
- A quick-fix, but a commitment; persistence and hard work are needed.
- A panacea or guarantee of success that can enhance human and financial resources, although they are still needed.
- Easy to do; but it is easy to understand and talk about.
- Dull, mechanical and boring; but rewarding and even fun.

A quality approach involves: client focus; thinking and planning ahead for the whole of the education institution; information gathering about problems in the system and sorting them out to prevent recurrences; being consistent and giving credit; admitting ignorance and seeking help; and saying thank you.[20] Perhaps the oft-cited remark by Robert Townsend says it all: 'If you can't do it excellently, don't do it at all'.[21]

In Chapter 3, attention turns to processes involved in accreditation of post-secondary education institutions and their programmes, as well as the *graduateness (job-readiness)* of individuals who enrol in them. The jargon merely ascribes some sense of achievement not only of a passing grade, but of a range of attributes and skills which have added value to the graduate for his or her future needs in life, including career and lifelong learning. Standards and evaluation are also addressed as they relate to quality management practices.

3

QUALITY ASSURANCE IN POST-SECONDARY EDUCATION: AN INTERNATIONAL OVERVIEW

Introduction

In this chapter an extensive review of the literature on accreditation, quality audits and standards is presented. Implications for individuals who graduate, especially those who seek licensure or registration to practise a profession, are explored. The global pursuit of quality assurance auditing of institutions and accrediting of programmes provides evidence of more mistakes made than lessons learned. An overview of the more predominant methods is provided to illustrate this point.

Accreditation and quality audit

Accreditation of educational programmes, which has been carried out in a variety of ways at various levels over the past 100 years or so in the industrialized Western world, has burgeoned and spread in the 1980s and 1990s to encompass almost all programmes and all levels of education, including post-secondary education. A *programme* is meant to define a set of courses or subjects or units which lead to graduation with a degree or certificate of some kind, and usually comprises a core curriculum and optional courses or subjects which students may choose.

The movement towards accreditation at the vocational and higher education level seems to have been generated by the political mood towards public accountability of the professions. In what terms can accreditation be defined? Cardozo says (paraphrasing Moliere), 'Accreditation is something like prose: a lot of people engage in it without realising what they are doing.'[1] Definitions of accreditation vary. In *Funk and Wagnalls New Encyclopedia* it is simply stated as the granting of approved status to an academic institution,[2] whereas the *Australian Oxford Mini Dictionary* defines *accredited*, somewhat tautologically, as holding credentials.[3] The *Universal English Dictionary* cites the Latin derivation of *credere* – to trust – and sees *accredit* as investing with credit, or sanctioning.[4] The *World Book Dictionary* defines *accreditation* as recognizing that a school, college, hospital or professional agency meets an official standard.[5] This latter definition clearly identifies a major problem for accreditation: that is, the need to meet something designated as a standard which is official. Such a definition begs the question: what is official? It is evident that in terms of function, standards may provide a benchmark for training providers, industry, training bodies and educators, or state and federal authorities. Standards may also be applied in considering individuals for registration, certification and other forms of recognition of skills, for setting curricula and in assessment of various kinds. Thus they may be linked to accreditation.

Although accreditation may have evolved from a perceived need to meet standards, it remains a poorly understood process, and a term described by Pinkham as 'elusive, nebulous [and] jellyfish'.[6] Young states that 'Accreditation has never been well understood – not by the general public nor, for that matter, by the institution of post-secondary education it primarily serves',[7] and provides the following definition which is generally accepted:

> accreditation is a process by which an institution of postsecondary education periodically evaluates *its own* educational activities, in whole or in part, and seeks an independent judgement that it substantially achieves its own educational objectives and is generally equal to comparable institutions or specialised units. Essential elements of the process are:
>
> 1 a clear statement of educational objectives;
> 2 a directed self-study focused on these objectives;
> 3 an on-site evaluation by a selected group of peers;
> 4 a decision by an independent commission that the institution or specialised unit is worthy of accreditation.[8]

Chernay gives a concise report of the history of this educational phenomenon, which was uniquely American when it evolved at the beginning of this century.[9] Institutional accreditation resulted when colleges and schools in various regions of the USA formed associations which developed standards that were generally recognized and accepted. As well, these associations were concerned about issues such as admission to graduate education, transfer of credit and articulation with secondary schools. The standards developed were utilized in a form of accreditation which was prescriptive, and required the reporting of data quantitatively. Because this early accreditation process did not take into account the needs and diversity of institutions, alterations to the methodology, from a simple set of tests or criteria to consideration of institutional and personal characteristics and qualities, were readily agreed upon. In the 1930s, standards for accreditation focused on the educational objectives and mission of the institution, *not, as previously, on fixed characteristics*. Thus, by the 1930s, accreditation included qualitative aspects.[10] The original motivation of idealism in developing cross-creditation and comparable standards was overtaken and exploited by certain socio-political forces concerned with funding.[11] This situation may be equated to the accountability model, which is evident as a pervasive force today.[12]

Beliefs about accreditation

The content and purpose of any set minimum standards, any criteria and any regulations are likely to be of differing value and significance to the different forces, which are conventionally termed stakeholders. There is evidence that, for an audit or accreditation process, this is especially so when there is legal or financial impact from not meeting the standards.[13]

There seems to be consensus that conducting a process of accreditation should provide a means of recognizing some level of performance, quality and integrity which engenders confidence from the public and the broad educational community.[14] This consensus may be the accumulation of some commonly held beliefs about the process.

The first belief is that accreditation is purported to provide quality assessment which is monitored by bodies assessing quality in post-secondary education, including governmental agencies and professional associations. It is claimed that the process of accreditation is undertaken in order to evaluate an institution or programme against some (not clearly articulated) minimally acceptable standards, which protect the institutions themselves, their students and the public.[15] Employers, business and industry may seek institutions and programmes that are accredited as a source of employees, continuing education programmes, joint research projects, foundations and the like. Public regard for being accredited may be seen to enhance the reputation of institutions and programmes. In the case of professional accreditation, the procedures could provide a means for practitioner involvement: (a) in the setting of entry-level standards, thereby providing a contribution to professional preparation programmes, as well as achieving a sense of ownership of the standards; (b) in the accreditation process itself; and (c) in providing a possible means of assurance of quality in the profession.[16]

A second belief, owing to Selden and Porter, is that quality should be assured through maintenance of minimum standards.[17] Thus, having undertaken a process of accreditation may imply that the institution or programme has clearly defined appropriate educational objectives, that it maintains the conditions under which there is reasonable expectation of meeting these objectives and that it can be expected to continue to meet them.

A third belief about the function attributed to accreditation is the fostering of excellence by developing criteria to enable the assessment of educational effectiveness. Accreditation functions to stimulate institutions and programmes to aspire to, and achieve, quality enhancement. It may be possible, by encouraging continuous review and self-study, and assisting developing and existing institutions and programmes through accreditation, to aim for continued updating and improvement. Thereby, accreditation may be much more than a means to achieve a status, and may foster excellence.

Finally, and an important implication, is a fourth belief that accreditation may also be the means whereby an institution can establish eligibility for funding and student assistance at both federal and state government levels.[18]

In summary, these beliefs claim that accreditation or quality audit serves public, educational and professional needs, and is a means to maintain and enhance the quality of standards, yet does not compromise the integrity of individual institutions and programmes.

Problems for accreditation

Despite these idealistic beliefs, there are likely to be tensions. First, there is evidence that institutions demand that their diverse and unique character and that of their programmes is maintained, despite, and in conjunction with, accreditation or audit processes.[19] Further, there is a strong sense of a demand that the ability and freedom to determine objectives, to be innovative and to resist undue external influences should not be hindered by accreditation or audit.

There is a second tension as governments impose more and more uniformity. We may suspect that the elements of reform, need and desire for improvement, voluntary action of professional groups, individualism, self-motivation, idealism and distrust of governments' motives (while acknowledging their ultimate power), which were motives for the process evident in the early days of accreditation, and which gave rise to any beliefs about it, are beliefs still honoured and its *raison d'être* today, and form the basis of argument for a move to auditing quality.

Why conduct accreditation?

To clarify where and by whom accreditation is undertaken, it is necessary to focus on the range of both the levels of accreditation and the agencies involved. Accreditation may be undertaken at different organizational or structural levels. For instance, it may be undertaken at the level of the institution or the programme and across a whole profession at a local, national or international level. At an individual level, graduates from accredited programmes may be assessed as part of individual licensure or registration which goes beyond the programme. The range of terms used in licensure and registration will be defined and discussed later.

Accrediting an institution of post-secondary education includes the accrediting of the total operating unit – that is, its management, level of physical and financial resources, and range of student personnel services, as well as the programmes which convey the content. It is generally agreed that, in order to make comparisons among institutions and in relation to specified criteria, policy on the description of institutions, in beginning an accreditation, requires that they all describe themselves in identical terms when applying for accreditation from any accrediting body. Furthermore, this is the case when applying in other countries, and despite the belief about accreditation catering for diversity.[20] Specifically, all institutions need to provide details about their purpose or mission, governance, programmes, degrees, diplomas, certificates, finances, personnel and constituents.

Accountability

Accountability is not only about educational programmes being seen to meet their own mission and goals, and those of their institution, but also about enhancement. Dinham and Evans discuss the concerns about educational quality which began in the 1980s. They comment on the external forces which impose demands. These include social trends, institutional forces, national reports and political pressures.[21]

No longer can educational accreditation be somewhat cosily claimed to be a voluntary process in which the decision-makers themselves are not held accountable.

There are some interesting discoveries in more recent literature and events which are related to the issue of accountability. Reitherman suggests in a recent article that, although the American College of Radiology's accreditation is voluntary, there is a market advantage to those who become involved. He also mentions the strong social, political and financial forces which are behind accreditation in all areas, not only in education.[22] In Australia, quality, excellence and improvement have become keywords in the educational policies of all political parties.[23]

It was affirmed in Chapter 1 that there are a range of views on quality, including: an essential attribute or characteristic; grade of excellence; fineness; merit[24] and degree or level of excellence; something that is special in a person or thing.[25] Continuous quality improvement describes the integration of quality and management methods, procedures, concepts and beliefs into the culture of practice to bring about continuous improvement in standards.[26] This concept is similar to Deming's *total quality management* focus for industry, and each depends on the application of *quality indicators* for monitoring, assessment, action, evaluation and feedback, which are the elements in each of these concepts.[27] In many cases, concurrence on the validity of indicators is not achieved by practitioners, educators and assessors. To satisfy the requirements of those agencies and bodies providing funding for education, health care and the like, there have been attempts to provide more effective means of monitoring and assessing quality. A professional responsibility to provide such quality is being increasingly advanced; however, there is evidence to question the relationship between being accredited and an assurance of quality. For example, a study of accredited nursing homes (albeit not directly related to accreditation of educational programmes) found no significant relationship between accreditation status and indicators of quality.[28]

Standards ∎

Standards may be applied to provide criteria for evaluation purposes. They may be norm-referenced (as in relation to a *passing standard* set previously by a group of examiners), task-referenced (as in *objectives* stated for observable tasks such as *matching, naming, selecting, recognizing)* or criterion-referenced (as when a *performance* is *compared* with stages on a scale of increasing competence).

In terms of function, standards may provide a *benchmark* or basic goal for training providers, industry and training bodies, or educators, as well as state and federal authorities. They may be applied in considering registration, certification, accreditation and other forms of recognition of skills, or for setting curricula and in assessment of various kinds. Standards can be expressed in different ways. It may be suggested that consideration be given to a number of factors when setting any level. These include:

- their eventual use;
- the audiences;
- operational and cultural requirements;
- the range of workplace and occupational situations.

How standards are set

There appear to be a number of methods identified in the literature concerning how standards are set, including various types of criterion-referenced, minimal competency and objective setting methods. In all cases, attention to reliability, validity, errors of measurement, test development and revision, scaling, norming, comparability and so on are given. Oral, written, multiple-choice or practical task tests may be used in assessment, so standards are set and evaluated to reflect the relevant methodology.

Livingstone and Zieky report on the Nedelsky style of setting minimally acceptable performance levels for multiple-choice assessment.[29] Judges (a panel of experts) consider together the questions and the level of knowledge (or skill) required to practise competently at an imaginary baseline of bare proficiency. Five or more judges discuss their particular concept of what is borderline or bare competence, using illustrative cases, until a consensus is reached. The score expected is thence derived from an agreed number of choices the minimally competent person should be able to make (for example, three out of the five alternatives).

Another procedure, the borderline group method, requires judges to use their knowledge of candidates (for example, in an educational or in a workplace setting) to judge whether they have a minimal level of knowledge or skill. Scores of this group may be used in defining minimum competence, and perhaps the median score used as a cut-off level.

A third procedure involves the contrasting of groups. This method similarly seeks judgement, but about each candidate as seen to be competent or incompetent. A means of defining a cut-off score may be found by smoothing a curve obtained from a plot of percentages of those deemed competent, and setting the score at the mid-point.

A fourth method, proposed by Angoff and cited in Thorndike, can be used with other than multiple-choice questions. Each judge considers the probability between 0.00 and 1.00 of someone minimally competent correctly answering the question. A minimum overall score is determined by summing this information over all questions.[30] There are other less well known methods, such as the *reference group method*, which requires comparison of one group, such as professionals from another country where different methods or levels of training are used, with a second group, in this instance those professionals trained in the country using the reference group method to determine the standard of overseas practitioners.

Caveats on setting standards

Glass provides a salutary lesson in avoiding assumptions about standard setting. He alludes to the *ad hoc* decisions made in determining standards or mastery levels in all the identified methods.[31] He remarks on the 1962 work of Mager, who claimed that the identification of standard setting is vital to stating objectives,[32] a proposition which Glass feels is less than meaningful – even meaningless! He also refers to the work of other authors, and urges caution in rigorously following Bloom's notion of *mastery learning*, as well as that of *performance standards* as espoused by Popham and Tyler.[33] Whatever the method of standard setting chosen, Glass asks us to consider the gap between desired performance and actual correct response rates when determining performance standards, and to avoid the assumption that setting standards will ensure that objectives are met.

The use of criterion-referenced testing, as described by Meskauskas, may also come under such scrutiny and begs that careful consideration be given to any discrepancies.[34] The term *criterion* may be alternated with *standard*, although, as we shall see, injudiciously. Glaser first couched the term *criterion-referenced tests* and suggested they be used to establish cut-off scores between competency and incompetency. In essence, criterion-referenced is to be applied to those tests constructed (and designed) to define rules which interrelate behavioural factors and test performance as criteria without the use of mathematical determinants to equate or relate to a cut-off score or standard.[35]

Glass also questions the use of the term *minimal competence*, which suggests the *essential, least permissible* level.[36] This appears on a continuum from absence to something especially excellent, and is extremely difficult to determine. In fact, judges disagree when seeking to determine these levels of *minimal competence*, and psychologically there is no basis for the concept. Placing a focus upon desired competencies for a particular profession may, however, offer a means by which a new or existing curriculum can be evaluated, particularly if the competencies have been defined in relation to the current needs in professional practice.[37] While educators may have specified their objectives carefully, the defining of needed competencies may present an opportunity for a more integrated approach to teaching, learning and student assessment.[38]

While acknowledging the arbitrary nature of standard setting, Scriven suggests that this is better than nothing at all.[39] Glass, in contrast, feels that 'arbitrariness is no bogeyman', yet that 'nothing is safer'.[40] So the argument is about the absolute nature of standards. In order to make a judgement about the value of anything or of anyone's performance, then some agreed level (with safety margins) may need to be determined or set.

Although most issues perceived to be *quantitative* have a *qualitative* basis, the notion of standard setting is more difficult in qualitative issues than in quantitative ones. Ambiguity may exist where competence can be expressed only in higher-order cognitive skill terms. The holistic nature of performance cannot be ignored. Consideration of some means of expressing the need for performance to be based on the combination of knowledge, skills, abilities and attributes poses a problem for those setting standards.

Norcini *et al.* report the results of two studies on standard setting in a range of professions. In one study it was found that specialization does not affect borderline group performance, which is heartening for those in professions where a narrow focus may preclude the retention of skills in all areas. The second study supported the provision of performance data during standard setting to ensure that item indices matched estimates of borderline group performance. Thus errors in pass/fail decisions were minimized.[41]

Competency-based standards

Since the major purpose of performance standards is to assist in decision-making, when setting the standards and in suggesting their application there is a need to attend to societal as well as political, ethical and other relevant factors.[42] Illustrations of some of these suggested applications have been provided by Chidley and Kisner, Nethery, and Ellingham and Fleischaker.[43] Curriculum development of undergraduate education using competency statements was described by Chidley and Kisner, who have demonstrated the capacity for cooperative involvement with other health professional education programmes when competency statements form the basis for curriculum design.[44] This particular application follows in the tradition of competency-based teacher education which has been promoted in the USA since the early 1970s.[45] Both Nethery and Ellingham and Fleischaker emphasize the usefulness of documented competencies in relation to clinical practice, especially from a quality assurance perspective.[46]

However, as suggested by Davis *et al.*, such competency-based standards may be based on outcomes and not related to inputs such as the traditional curricula employed in education.[47] In any case, Rancourt and Ballantine argue that the application of competencies to the education process in health areas requires a shift away from the more generally accepted subject-based curriculum and epistemic orientation models of education.[48] The subject-based curriculum assumes that knowledge of the required subject matter, without it being linked to professional practice, will enable the student to perform the various professional tasks at the appropriate level.[49] The extent to which this is likely to be achieved requires careful consideration, as outlined by Bullock, and Shepard and Jensen.[50] The epistemic orientation model is predicated on the notion that knowledge is acquired according to an individual mental construction which results from the channelling of cognitive abilities in a particular educational environment, and therefore contains difficulties in making standards explicit.[51] On the other hand, the competence-based curriculum identifies the components of the various tasks required of the beginning practitioner, and establishes educational experiences which will enable the student to gain these specific competencies.[52] This information is included to highlight the dilemmas and difficulties in the area of competence and standards.

Burton suggests that it is difficult to determine minimal competency for reasons that are inherent in real-life success or failure. In her paper, it is purported that no single skill is as essential as needed for survival. As well, there is discussion about the requirements of such abilities as hearing and reading as basic to many skills. While Burton agrees that having skills is good, and that the more one has, the greater the chances of survival and success, she does not see that some skills are so necessary that they should be made *standards*.[53]

Objectives and standards

Objectives tend to be expressions of what is desired in terms of outcomes, without alluding, necessarily, to a level or standard to be achieved. Indeed, objectives may address the same matters and issues that lend themselves to the development of standards. These are areas of knowledge and skills in the cognitive domain, as well as the affective domain of attitudes and values.[54] Motor skills of gross and fine manipulation and eye–hand coordination are usually also addressed.

The main difference between an objective and a standard is that an objective itself may identify the means by which the objective may be seen to be met, and a standard requires that additional information sources, such as performance criteria, need to be provided, and the level at which they are to be met specified. For example, in relation to knowledge, *objectives* may be developed in a variety of areas, such as *knowing where to find information*. For this objective:

- a means of *achieving* this objective may be having a lecture from a librarian;
- a means of *evaluating whether the objective has been met* may be indirect evidence from essays and/or examination answers.[55]

A *standard* in the area of knowledge may seek to ensure that performance criteria are met at a specific level, not in a global way. In fact, the only essential difference between an objective and a standard is that for a standard there is the concept of a *set level*: for example, minimal competence, mastery and the like. Since the setting of standards requires use of judgement, past experience and exemplars, the process may be countered with opposing judgements, experience and exemplars. Moreover, the standards may need to be lowered sufficiently so that they can be met by everyone. Objectives may be more simplistically met, and anyone who does not meet them is not seen as *substandard* but as having *not yet met the objectives*. A moot point.

Perhaps standard is an alternative word used to set a level, where formal examination or evaluation cannot ensure that an objective has been met. In any event, both objectives and standards require agreed conventions, and professional judgement in which there may be disagreement about decisions when it comes to scoring, and passing or failing.

The use of standards

Standards may be deemed to be necessary by governments: for example, to enable industrial groups, unions, registration boards and the like to ensure that all workers, employees, professionals or practitioners meet a minimum standard of performance in a range of skills and abilities.[56] Educationalists and professional bodies may set standards for the training or education of personnel.[57] These should match the minimum standard required by a newly qualified or graduated trainee or professional. Where quality assurance is required or desired, standard setting means that there is a reference point against which to judge the quality and ensure that it is maintained.

Accreditation and quality audit has changed from using only quantitative criteria to demonstrate that a standard has been met, to incorporating more qualitative criteria and encouraging institutions to maintain their individuality. The use of self-study, self-evaluation and self-regulation is evident as a part of the process, but it is suggested that the understanding of accreditation is based more on beliefs about what it is than on any reality about its nature.

Public regard for being accredited may be seen to enhance the reputation of institutions, programmes and curricula. Stakeholders such as governments, the international education community and potential students are interested in knowing whether there are:

• clearly defined, educationally appropriate objectives;
• positive graduate outcomes;
• conditions which ensure continuous improvement.[58]

Validation of specific (professional) courses is the term used in the UK and EU synonymously with accreditation elsewhere. Indeed, graduation from a validated or accredited course assures registration of health professionals. In professional accreditation, therefore, there is a need to set standards which protect the institutions themselves, their students and the public. Ownership of such standards by the profession contributes to the provision of a means of assuring quality in the profession itself.

Linking standards and education

At the programme level, any educational programmes accredited in conjunction with an institution may be accredited as either liberal or general studies, or in terms of their profession-specific standards: for example, the accreditation of arts or science programmes in contrast to programmes preparing individuals to enter professions such as engineering or medicine. Accreditation at the programme level within or in affiliation with institutions may also apply to schools, departments or single purpose institutes which prepare professionals and technicians.

The range of accrediting agencies involved at the level of the profession as a whole includes multipurpose and individual professional commissions and committees. Their responsibility is to fields in which, in addition to academic proficiency, profession-specific competence and ethical and public concerns apply to health, welfare and safety issues.[59] Any standards for such specialized accreditation should be developed through cooperation between practitioners, educators, consumers and other stakeholders, such as education institutions, employers and public agencies. These standards would then ideally be applied to assess the inputs and outcomes which obtain to meet the objective of satisfactory quality. Thus the expectations and requirements for the professional entering and practising in the field of specialization may be specified, and any quality standards identified would be used in accrediting the adequacy of any education programme preparing the professional. Specialized accrediting bodies may accredit the programme, but would not make judgements about the institution (unless it is single purpose for a specific profession).

There is a complex interplay between accreditation, authoritative demands of governments and professions, as well as integration of quality and access issues. Ensuring diversity and preserving standards requires careful management.[60]

Finally, yet another level of accreditation is becoming a factor. There is a move to consider international standards of accreditation for some professions. However, this move introduces many complicating issues, including culture, secondary education level and standards, language, terminology, finances, resources, expectations and outcomes.[61] Formation of the Global Alliance for Transnational Education (GATE) may assist in resolving some of these issues, although there is little evidence so far that this is the case.[62]

The complications are highlighted when comparability is distinguished from equivalency. A discussion on international accreditation addresses some form of recognition which may be granted to foreign education institutions or programmes. Clarification of what the parameters of recognition might be is given. It is suggested that some form of recognition that is not accreditation may be granted: 'A lesser standard such as comparability and not equivalency should be considered a different status than accreditation'.[63] The terms used add to the confusion about what granting accreditation means. The idea that an institution may undergo an accreditation process but not be granted accreditation throws the situation into further confusion. Such a significant discrepancy begs addressing and clarification by those involved in the international accreditation process.

'Graduateness'

Professional accreditation – assessing whether programmes produce graduates who meet entry-level competency standards – is more closely linked to eligibility for registration. It may be that the only reliable means of assessing whether health professionals (for example) seeking to register initially meet the entry-level competency standards is for them to undertake an examination. In Australia, the use of competency standards as part of a process of accreditation of health professionals' education programmes is undergoing informed debate prior to the consideration of any implementation.[64] This is timely in view of the focus of the Australian federal government on auditing quality procedures in higher education, which requires education institutions and programmes to have quality assurance processes in place.

There are political, professional and social mandates which call for greater accountability, and this is particularly the case in all the health professions. Such accountability is required not only in practice, but also in the education of medical and allied health practitioners. Changing population demographies see increasing numbers of elderly people, with political health care moves demanding more community-based services in order to save limited funds by keeping patients at home, or at least out of acute hospital beds. These factors have implications for the numbers taken into educational programmes, and the relevance of these programmes for the training of health professionals.[65]

Current health profession education programmes may be reviewed through a variety of activities. Such activities are usually termed accreditation or validation, they may take place every five to ten years, may be internal, external or combined and may be conducted by reviewers with no or dubious experience and expertise in the area of accreditation or evaluation. Furthermore, although the ultimate aim of the education programmes is to prepare competent entry-level clinicians, the standard of competence for each clinical skill is known only to individual schools. Indeed, no significant correlation between individuals' grades and clinical competence has been found.[66] Australian health professionals have only recently developed a set of agreed clinical standards or competencies which may be useful in the future for accrediting the content of programmes, as well as for assessing the provision of health care.[67]

There are a vast and growing number of accrediting agencies, which undertake institutional or professional accreditation, especially in the USA. In the USA and the UK, accrediting and auditing agencies, while undertaking different types of processes, cooperate to the extent that any site visits may be concurrent where institutional affiliations exist, or where international accrediting bodies are involved with any one profession. There are institutional concerns about the number of accrediting agencies, types of accreditation and difficulty level of standards to be met.[68] The financial and legal implications of accreditation of any type can lead to administrators expressing the fear that they may be held hostage, especially by professional accreditation bodies. In the USA, the Pew Health Professions Commission has looked at health care and how changes impact on health professional practice, education and regulation.[69] In particular, the Commission has looked at how accreditation may assist schools to meet the requirements of these changes.

Terminology

An article by Kandor and Bobby highlights the confusion in terminology in accreditation and the need for clear definition by those who use the various terms. Just as the terminology on accreditation is complex, so is the terminology on individuals.[70] When the assessment of the educational process moves from considering institutions and programmes to considering the competence of individuals, then the word accreditation is no longer used. It is interesting to look at the use of three different terms: *licensure, certification* (both of which are linked to registration) and *credentialing.*

Licensure

Universities developed in Europe in the 1100s, in most instances from teachers' guilds in cathedral schools. In the middle ages, passing examinations was a requirement for judging a *master*, or highly skilled craftsman, in a *guild* or association of those with common interests. In this context, the guilds (chiefly of merchants and craftsmen) were the beginnings of professional associations, and thereby, the masters were the precursors to professionals.[71]

Licensure for professions evolved from the conducting of examinations to determine which practitioners could become masters, but did not begin in the USA, for example, until the nineteenth century.[72] Before that time, individuals could practise medicine without any formal qualifications. Within the leadership of the medical fields in this period, there was a feeling for the need to distinguish between those practitioners who had undertaken specific professional training and those who had not, and with a view to protecting the public, licensing laws were developed. As a result of professional pressure, medical and other professional boards were then set up to administer the laws. Subsequently, codes of conduct, standards of practice and methods to screen applicants were developed. Licensure for individuals is necessary across a range of occupations (more than 800 in the USA), and by and large is a matter for states in that country. Licensure is available to many professionals in other countries.

Certification

Certification may be awarded as an alternative to licensure, usually as the result of an examination. This is often conducted by a body representing a range of professions (for example, the Board of Registry in the USA, representing 17 associations of laboratory science professions).[73] Moreover, Berggren defines certification as the 'process of reviewing the educational experiences and measuring the knowledge and skills of individuals'.[74] This procedure is separate from accreditation, which is an activity undertaken for institutions and programmes at a national level. Certification for some occupational groups, such as hairdressers and plumbers, is available similarly in other countries, but to a lesser extent.

Credentialing

A further term used, primarily in the USA, is credentialing, which refers to the competencies of an individual. It is not in common use in other countries. There is a link between accreditation and supplying with credentials. Indeed, Loesch sees credentialing as being comprised of programme accreditation, certification and licensure.[75]

To summarize, various manuals containing information on how to conduct accreditation have been produced to help accreditors to carry out their task. The manuals are restricted to describing and prescribing, in a step-by-step fashion, the procedures to be followed.

Outcomes in accreditation

Accreditation of curricula is facilitated by the identification of intended outcomes. Merely crossing off items on a checklist may be validation of criteria being addressed in the programme or by the institution, but cannot assure quality or provide credit for any of them. Focusing on whether the outcomes have been achieved or exceeded provides a means for those accrediting curricula to avoid pedantry and look at the curriculum as a structured series of intended learning outcomes.[76] The series necessarily includes outcomes related to:

1 Knowledge: facts, concepts and generalizations (laws, principles).
2 Techniques (processes, abilities, skills): cognitive and psychomotor.
3 Values: norms and predilections.

Furthermore, the curriculum should demonstrate that the sources for content are comprehensive and valid in terms of available culture, disciplinary inquiry and non-disciplinary experience. Other factors, such as *teachability* (implying *learnability*) and ideology (including values, utility, significance), are of interest. A range of methodologies to cater for different learning styles, as well as flexibility in instruction and assessment, should be evident. Inclusion of meta-evaluation by instructors as well as internal reviews of all aspects of the programme, not only the curriculum, is expected. Operationalizing the terms of reference for a review group involved in accreditation generally results in formulation of a range of questions about the programme.

An example is provided in the accreditation process for medical schools in Australia and New Zealand undertaken by the Australian Medical Council (AMC). The objectives for the programmes in relation to knowledge and understanding, and skills and attitudes as they affect professional behaviour, are defined in general terms. Likewise, an outline of the institutional settings, resources and approaches required to achieve the objectives are described. The curriculum is defined only in broad outline.[77]

In a paper titled 'Thirteen steps to outcomes accreditation: Maine West's experience', Paul Leathem presents a procedure used at Maine West High School in Des Plaines, Illinois.[78] It is not the intention to detail the steps here, but Leathem reports that this type of accreditation has been a source of learning for those involved. There has been a possibility to look more closely at what is being taught in relation to what is learnt, and how it is learnt. By assessing student performance and setting goals, instructional strategies could be planned to improve student performance, and changes in the outcomes could be measured. This important development in the assessment of outcomes may be a means to reconcile the legal, social and political implications which may result from denying accreditation to a programme. Moreover, this development may be a further motivation for the assessment of individuals after they graduate.

Common elements in accreditation models

There is a range of models incorporating sets of criteria and desirable characteristics of graduates which may be considered in evaluating the curriculum as part of an accreditation process. These include:

1 Typology, programmatic and outcomes models.
2 Clusters of criteria related to programme philosophy, faculty qualifications, programme context, curriculum philosophy, field experience or practicum, student competencies, quantitative approaches
  and diversity of courses.
3 Characteristics of graduates including coherent and extensive knowledge in a discipline area, logical reasoning to distinguish fact from
  opinion, appreciation of others' cultures and customs, clear communication and fluent writing skills, oral articulation and confidence,
  and computer literacy.[79]

In summary, the common elements found among accreditation models are:

The programme
General
  Mission
  Philosophy
Content
  Substantive knowledge
  Intellectual skills
  Professional skills

Antecedents
Students
  Prior knowledge
  Entry requirements
  Pastoral care
  Other guidance
Faculty
  Qualifications
  Experience

Transactions
Teaching
Learning
Research
Operational
  Fair practice
  Equal opportunity

Outcomes
Immediate
  Graduation criteria
Intermediate
  Registration or certification
  Competence to practise

Assessment
Programme
  Internal
  External
Students
  Assessment methods
  Assessment criteria

Physical aspects
Resources
  Financial
  Facilities
  Equipment
  Supplies
  Intellectual
    Library
    Audio-visual
    Computing
Personnel
  Administrative
  Clerical and other support
  Technical
  Faculty
    Academic
    Clinical

From this summary of common elements it is evident that accreditation contains two classes of elements, though these are not equally represented. First, there are those which may be called *input* elements, such as the content of programmes, the range of students who come into them, the commitment and quality of faculty, the range of physical resources and other personnel available to the programme, the duty of care owed to students and faculty and consideration of the mission and philosophy of the institution and the programme. Formative and summative evaluation of teachers and departments may be included here.[80]

Second, although less evident, is a class of elements which are related to *outcomes*. These concern the assessment of the teaching and learning that takes place, graduation criteria and the number of students who graduate from the programmes.

The clear separation of inputs from outcomes, and the emphasis on the former in most accreditation models, provides the clue to understanding why accreditation rarely fails (totally). The provision of programmes is very much a socio-political matter. The political difficulties associated with loss of funding, credibility and therefore closure of a programme would not only seriously disadvantage current students and faculty, but also have implications for the institution, past students and faculty and the society which they serve. Therefore, where there are deficiencies in input elements, the choice is to identify them as matters to be rectified, not as a programme to be eliminated. This can be carried out because it is possible to overcome a deficit in input elements by making changes to staff, physical resources and even the students taken into a programme.

In contrast, because the socio-political consequences are not as explicit, it may not be as easy to make changes in the outcomes elements. This explains, at least in part, why less attention is paid to them by decision-makers. To some extent, the focusing on inputs implies that the outcomes arising from the inputs can be taken for granted. That is, if the inputs are in place, then the required outcomes will follow. However, there is a potential for a tremendously large gap here, and it is necessary to check that the required outcomes are also in place.

Stufflebeam and Webster succinctly expressed similar observations: 'The main difficulties are that the guidelines of accrediting and certifying bodies typically emphasize the intrinsic and not the outcome criteria of education'.[81]

Summarizing accreditation

Perhaps accreditation can only be considered as a process of developing and maintaining some level of quality (which in itself is difficult to define and quantify), and some level of resourcing, curriculum and the like. Furthermore, to be accredited has little to do with assessing those levels with any degree of accuracy or comparability because of the structure of educational accreditation, which at this time is poorly understood. This revelation is not a cause to abandon accreditation, but has to be reflected in the theory which has been enunciated by Liston, and in the structure which has been clarified in the same study.[82] The evolving quality assurance audit processes around the globe have provided only marginally greater clarity on how a level of quality can be assessed.

The relationship between higher education and society is changing, with more emphasis on producing employable graduates. Furthermore, with greater enrolments in post-secondary education, national budgets are stretched. The danger is that quality will be threatened if efficiency is the focus. Attention to the added value and benefits of post-secondary education cannot be ignored. Accountability and assurance of quality is an international societal demand, with assessments and audits of quality both internally and externally being common practice in post-secondary education worldwide.

Although accreditation serves multiple customers, it should be responsive to the expressed interests of the real consumers, not interests that are interpreted by accreditors. Maintaining the *status quo* through accreditation may serve short-term interests, but will not foster opportunities for continuous improvement and maintaining diversity.[83] Leaders in post-secondary education institutions, professions and licensing or registration bodies must decide on what value is added by the processes of accreditation and quality audit. The focus should always be on improving the outcomes and impact for all stakeholders.

International overview of quality assurance methods and agencies

Born in the USA

To provide a form of what in modern parlance would be termed *quality assurance* concerning the preparation and entry-level standards for professional practice, specialized accreditation grew from work in the area of medical education. Until 1949, little communication took place among the ever-increasing number of accrediting bodies in the USA. At that time the National Commission on Accrediting was established, and provided a review and recognition process for existing accrediting bodies.[84] The National Committee of Regional Accrediting Agencies was formed, to enhance communication, foster cooperation and develop common procedures and policies.[85] In 1969, this body became the Federation of Regional Accrediting Commissions of Higher Education, until it merged with the National Commission on Accrediting in 1975 to form the Council on Postsecondary Accreditation, which disbanded in 1992 when the International Network for Quality Assurance Agencies in Higher Education came into being.[86] Professional educators and associations developed, and continue to develop, definitions of the scope of their practice, as well as criteria and process procedures for eligibility for licensure or registration for practitioners, and for the purpose of undertaking educational accreditation. It is not the intention to provide a lengthy overview of quality assurance models here, but to mention some of the currently evolving national programmes.

In the USA, it appears that groups or agencies which establish the standards or criteria for accreditation are employed by institutions, professional associations and similar organizations to undertake accreditation on request. It is reported that these groups and agencies are non-governmental, voluntary, institutional or professional bodies which make public the information resulting from an accreditation exercise. In other countries, control of educational standards is, in the main, established and maintained at a national level by governments. Either way, accreditation status can influence funding agencies (government and private), scholarship commissions, employers, counsellors, advisors, students and potential students. There is evidence that the role and responsibility of accrediting bodies is seen to have become quasi-public and of concern to a range of groups associated in some way with education.[87]

The UK experience

In the UK, British post-secondary education came under scrutiny from the Council for National Academic Awards (CNAA) in 1964, when it was formed to monitor and guarantee quality and standards in the newly established polytechnic sector. From 1984 to 1986, reports (the Reynolds Reports and the Lindop Report) introduced formal quality assurance systems in universities, which were gradually transferred from the CNAA to individual institutions (under licence). Green provides an overview of progress through the Education Reform Act of 1988, when the polytechnics and colleges were incorporated and two new funding councils were established (the Universities Funding Council and the Polytechnics and Colleges Funding Council), to the Further and Higher Education Act of 1992, when the binary line was abolished. The CNAA was also abolished in 1992, and at that time the Higher Education Quality Council was formed.[88]

The Committee of Vice-Chancellors and Principals Academic Unit (CVCPAU) was established in 1990 to audit quality assurance processes in universities. In 1991, polytechnics were designated as universities. Quality assessment became a statutory responsibility for the Higher Education Funding Councils (HEFCs) which were established for England, Scotland and Wales in 1992 to replace the binary system's funding councils. Also in 1992, the Higher Education

Quality Council (HEQC) was established by universities to take over the audit role of the CVCPAU, and the access and quality enhancement roles of the CNAA. A tumultuous two years![89]

The HEQC for England began developing quality assessment methods in 1992, around the same time the Australian government set up the Committee for Quality Assurance in Higher Education. By 1995, the British process involved assessing curriculum design, content and organization; teaching, learning and assessment; student progression and achievement; student support and guidance; learning resources; quality assurance and enhancement.

Proposed significant cuts in higher education funding in the UK over the triennium 1996–9 created anger in an already unacceptably unstable sector and prompted the Dearing Review.[90] (Interestingly, the terms of reference were similar to those of the West Review in Australia.) In order to shape the long-term requirements for the nation, recommendations were sought on the purposes, structure, shape, size and funding of higher education. Alongside this review, the two functions of funding and quality assurance audit were themselves under review by a joint planning group which recommended a single agency to manage the functions of the HEFCs and the HEQC. The resulting Quality Assurance Agency (QAA) was established in 1998. The aims of the new system are:

1 To assess the extent to which institutions are monitoring and managing the quality of teaching and learning.
2 To evaluate the quality assurance system of each institution.
3 To identify areas of strength and weakness.
4 Generally to enhance the quality of higher education.

There is to be a cycle of external audits to monitor internal assessments and reviews.[91] There is already a cycle of external assessment of research, so the system may not ease the already troubled breasts of academics in the UK, where change is the only constant.

And in Australia

The Australian system of quality assurance assessments involved looking generally in 1993, at teaching and learning in 1994 and at research and community service in 1995. Each of these three rounds involved placing institutions in categories which attracted greater or lesser amounts of *quality funds*. By 1996 the funding stopped, and like the British system, moved to a process managed by the Higher

Education Council, which is linked more closely to funding through the Department of Employment, Education, Training and Youth Affairs.

In the Australian government's 1996 higher education budget statement the relevant minister announced an objective to meet Australia's social, cultural, economic and labour market demands for a more highly educated and skilled population by:

1 Establishing priorities and mechanisms for effective resource alloca-tion which reflect changing economic and social goals.
2 Maintaining and enhancing the quality of education provided by the higher education system and encouraging institutions to improve graduation rates.
3 Maintaining high participation at both undergraduate and post-graduate levels, within the context of balanced growth in post-compulsory education and training.
4 Encouraging the introduction and further development of meas-ures to increase equity of access to higher education, including flexible admission policies, credit transfer, support and bridging programmes.
5 Establishing a closer partnership between higher education institu-tions and industry.[92]

In the light of these objectives, sector-wide performance indicators are being developed. The aim of the government is to provide a quality assessment process that, as far as practicable, is hard edged through the application of quantitative performance indicators and benchmarks which are carefully selected and genuinely meaningful, and recognize institutional diversity. Institutions must have quality management plans and statements of strategic quality outcomes which are related to, or integrated with, each institution's plan. Quality reviews are built into the annual *profiles* process which is conducted in relation to funding. Desktop audits of outcomes against targets were proposed, with on-site visits every three to four years.

South Africa takes up the challenge

Dorothy Illing reported in *The Australian Higher Education Supple-ment* that in South Africa the reformation of the higher education sector is adopting a similar system of nationally funding universit-ies, technikons and colleges on a three-year rolling cycle. There is a Council on Higher Education with around 30 members, which has a committee responsible for quality and undertaking programme accreditation and institutional audits. Greater access for previously disadvantaged black students will need to be monitored as increasing numbers and variable standards on entry may see increased failure rates and high levels of drop-out. A thorough review of degrees, certificates and diplomas will be undertaken, with possibilities for mergers and closures.[93]

The South African Ministry of Education has a vision for the sector which will:

1 Promote equity of access and fair chances of success to all who are seeking to realize their potential through higher education, irrespective of race, colour, gender, creed, age or class.
2 Meet, through well planned and coordinated teaching and learning programmes, the high-skilled employment needs presented by a growing economy aspiring to global competitiveness.
3 Support a democratic ethos and culture of human rights by educational programmes and practices conducive to critical discourse and creative thinking, cultural tolerance and a common commitment to a humane, non-racist and non-sexist social order; contribute to the advancement of all forms of knowledge and scholarship, in keeping with international standards of academic quality, and with sensitivity to the diverse problems and demands of the local, national, southern African and African contexts.

There are a number of vexed issues facing South Africa and other African countries as they grapple with a paradigm shift in post-secondary education, which sees not only a greater focus on clients and service to clients, but changing demographic and contextual realities.

Whither Canada?

The Quebec government in Canada established a Commission for evaluating college education in 1993. Other provinces in Canada have their own quality assurance system, but there is no national process in place.[94] The process of appraisal of graduate programmes in Ontario Province was established by the Ontario Council on Graduate Studies in 1983 and is unique in North America. It is voluntary, but of interest to government. In 1997, a similar appraisal process for undergraduate programmes commenced in response to the 1992 Broadhurst Taskforce on Accountability report.[95]

China

With over 1000 institutes of higher learning, the State Education Commission of China embarked on a programme to evaluate university graduate schools in 1995. Of the 223 universities authorized to confer doctoral degrees, only 33 have approved graduate schools. The quality assurance system comprises a number of indices which are used to evaluate the quality of staff and the supervisory team, courses, quality and quantity of students, quality of theses and marking of them, awards, grants and so on. Judgements of experts are weighted by school, region and personnel in an attempt to achieve reliability – a developing system.[96]

Hong Kong

Hong Kong, on the other hand, introduced a performance-based funding model in 1994. Teaching and learning quality process reviews were conducted between September 1995 and April 1997 of the seven tertiary education institutions funded by the University Grants Committee of Hong Kong. A preliminary visit was made to each institution, which then prepared a 20-page document describing its quality assurance and improvement processes. Subsequently, there was a one and a half day audit visit from a review team to validate the evidence provided in the document. Teaching and learning processes in all seven institutions were found to be broadly satisfactory, examples of best practice were found and areas needing improvement were identified. Thus the process and outcomes are similar to most other established or evolving quality assurance audit and accreditation processes.[97]

Europe spreads a net

An important Directory of Advanced Training Opportunities in African, Caribbean and Pacific states is a project of the European Union. It was established to provide an overview of post-secondary programmes available to students in these states, who seek to study in other states, through assessing compliance with a range of quality standards based on ISO 9001 norms.[98]

The European pilot projects for evaluating quality in higher education were initiated by the European Commission in 1994. They involved the 15 member countries, Norway and Iceland, and concluded in 1995. In 1997, a European Network of Quality Assurance Agencies in Higher Education was established to bring together representatives from national and federal agencies in countries which have established evaluation procedures, and government representatives from those countries which do not have a national quality assurance system. There are members in the network from the university and non-university sectors. Eastern and Central European countries are connected as observers. So the quality assurance assessment net is being cast widely.[99]

In Bulgaria, a new Higher Education Act was passed at the end of 1995, and a National Evaluation and Accreditation Agency was put in place. Its functions are:

1 To develop, update and apply standards, quantitative and qualitative criteria and procedures, applicable to all institutions of higher education, state and private.
2 To provide information on the results of completed evaluation and accreditation procedures and their effect on quality improvement within both higher education and the training of highly skilled researchers.

Governed by an Accreditation Council, the Agency has 23 highly qualified members covering most fields of study. The model of quality assessment used is similar to that in the Netherlands, and has links with the British model of self-assessment and peer review.[100]

Similarly, the Swedish model focuses on quality enhancement through reports (since 1994) to a Higher Education Quality Council. Audits of the 36 state higher education institutions began in 1997 and were planned to be completed by 2000.[101]

The Netherlands moves internationally

In the Netherlands, where there is a binary system for post-secondary education, external quality assurance has been on the government's agenda since 1986, and has been a topic hotly debated in universities and professional colleges. A national and comparative approach by field of study was adopted and began in 1988. External quality assessments, which have been coordinated by the Association of Universities, have gone through two cycles. An international programme review process will replace the national comparative assessment for the third round in 2000.[102]

New Zealand moves to the next phase

The New Zealand Universities Academic Audit Unit was set up in early 1994 and completed its first cycle of external quality reviews for the seven universities at the end of 1997. The process of self-assessment and external audit is similar to those elsewhere. It is already under review for the second round, as are most other processes.[103]

Why? What next? Who are the beneficiaries? ▮

Although the preceding overview of accreditation and quality assurance processes is not exhaustive, it is clear that activity is increasing and changes in processes are often made for dubious reasons. While changes are necessary to cater for learning about review processes, changes to processes are less productive when imposed by the whims of the government of the day. As Woodhouse and others eloquently suggest, audits bring a shift in power from the well trusted (e.g. academics and teachers, doctors and other health professionals) to the less trusted (e.g. accountants and auditors) by the least trusted (politicians).

There is evidence that most of the models of quality assessment are moving to considering improvement, rather than merely validating or accrediting provision. Lee Harvey has been focusing for some time on transformation in learning.[104] Instilling reflective practice in teachers, a critical ability to move beyond well-established parameters and pathways in problem-solving in academics and students, and finding ways to link innovation to monitoring processes are his visions of a transformation of the learning paradigm. Indeed, he proposes a shift from quality in an *accountability* context to quality as *improvement* achieved through transformation. And why not? This notion is wise, sensible, reasonable and appealing, if not to governments, then certainly to academics.

Whether private or public, expensive and tedious accreditation and quality assurance models, which do not seek improvement as their primary purpose, are stifling diversity, not providing information about the quality of courses and service to clients and certainly demoralizing and infuriating academics and those who support teaching and research in post-secondary education.[105] Where is the value? Who benefits? Who audits the auditors and reports on the outcomes from their efforts? Are these activities fostering improvement? If not, they must quickly move to do so or be transformed. Thomas Kuhn would have applauded this paradigm shift as a notable scientific revolution.[106]

In Chapter 4 the focus moves to quality improvement – the principles, processes and tools which can be used. Measurements and varieties of evaluation models are also presented to assist readers to manage quality in their own post-secondary education institution. In addition, some of the costs and casualties of the quality movement are briefly visited.

4

QUALITY IMPROVEMENT IN EDUCATION ENVIRONMENTS

Introduction

Having visited the historical background to the quality movement, and reviewed the range of accreditation and quality assurance mechanisms undertaken in relation to post-secondary education, it is important to move to how the sector can apply quality improvement principles.

Not only is this chapter focusing on education environments, but it also brings the quality improvement debate to reality through providing practical examples applicable to the post-secondary education sector. It begins with a checklist of principles and a framework for a quality management system, then moves to describing processes. Models of review are presented to guide readers through a range of stages using lists of key elements. A number of quality tools are briefly outlined because they are useful in quality improvement activities.

To provide a broader perspective on standards and measurement in preparation for the ensuing chapters on benchmarking, best practice and the use of indicators, the historical evolution of models of evaluation in education is presented. A salient warning is given on injudicious implementation of quality systems as add-ons for certification to standards rather than as day-to-day practice.

Principles

It was W. Edwards Deming who asserted, empirically, that unless quality was measured, it could not be improved. The pre-eminent principle for quality management is not control but improvement.

Assuring quality is about conformity and reproducibility. The concept does not sit well in education where individual students and teachers, and variability in methodologies (even if content is prescribed), provide enhancement to the learning experience and foster diversity. However, improvement relies on attention to the three elements of a simple quality process model introduced by Deming in 1986 in his book *Out of the Crisis*.[1] These are input → throughput → output. He espoused the principle that efficiency and effectiveness influence success and survival. While equity is a paramount issue, there is no doubt that variability in the knowledge-base and skills of entering students is a factor likely to affect interactions between students, and between students and academics during their programmes, thus influencing the outcomes.[2]

In designing a system for managing quality the focus must be on the core business of the organization, and on client needs. Furthermore, it must be useful. Flexibility and applicability will assist in achieving a genuine desire by everyone to take responsibility for caring about improving performance as their purpose.[3]

So, what is a *quality* system? One that demonstrates that it includes:

1 A mission, goals and objectives that are clear and are communicated to all.
2 Systems that are well planned and coordinated, and communicated to all.
3 Shared responsibility which has been communicated to all.
4 Quality indicators which are well defined, documented and communicated to all.
5 Monitoring and measurement systems in place for verification, and which are communicated to all.
6 Methods to correct errors which have been communicated to all.[4]

In the post-secondary education sector the following principles provide a framework for a quality management system to foster improvement:

- the chief executive officer (president or vice-chancellor) and executive managers are responsible for leading in the advancement of quality through monitoring and review to identify best practice using agreed *key performance indicators* (KPIs);
- commitment to quality is necessary for all elements of the education institution;
- everyone is responsible for continuous quality improvement in the workplace;

- quality management principles are incorporated into operational unit (faculty, school, department) plans;
- adequate resources are available to support quality management processes.

Characteristics of effective quality management are:

- planning, innovation and strategies to implement change;
- use of benchmarks, standards and KPIs for monitoring change;
- evaluation of best practice for continuous improvement;
- efficiency and cost-effectiveness;
- relational management information systems and reporting mechanisms;
- dissemination of information and ongoing communication.

Processes

By reviewing their own mission and goals in the light of the institution's vision, mission, values, goals and objectives (e.g. for teaching and learning, research, international and community interactions), staff in each operational unit, school and department will share in setting a standard against which achievements are to be judged. Improvement can be gauged through regular review using agreed criteria. The processes of review may be five- or six-yearly for entire programmes to inform long-term planning, or annual reviews against short-term targets. They form part of a typical *quality cycle* (see Figure 4.1).

Programme and planning reviews

The institution's strategic planning and review processes are the framework for quality improvement, planning and evaluation of initiatives across the entire organization.

A process of self-assessment, external validation and strategic planning provides a means by which staff and students may develop a shared sense of purpose, as well as greater and improved understanding of the directions in which the operational unit wishes to go. The outcomes of this exercise include:

1 Identification of strengths, weaknesses and operations to be changed.
2 Ownership of strategies determined as necessary to strengthen distinctive niches and to make changes vital to the ability to demonstrate improvement.

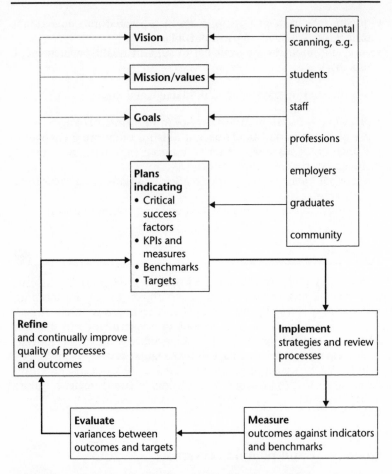

Figure 4.1 Sample of an education institution quality cycle.

Overall, when undertaking a five- or six-yearly review, each operational unit will be better able to further the achievement of the institution's mission, goals and objectives by:

1 Addressing relevant strategies determined in teaching and learning, research and other plans.
2 Considering value commitments and belief statements.
3 Identifying their own purpose and direction.

A six-yearly rolling cycle of reviews fits well with a three-yearly

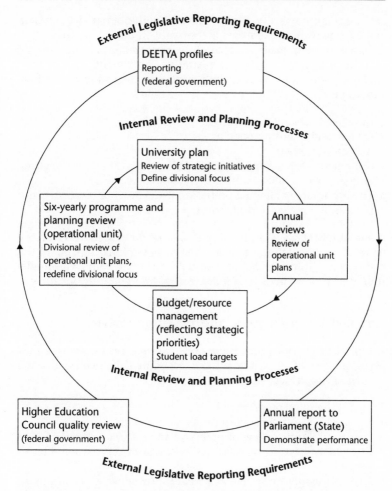

Figure 4.2 Example of a cycle for planning and review.

rolling budget cycle, which is current practice in some countries where education institutions rely on government funding. Plans should be reviewed during the programme review process and can be referred to by bodies responsible for the institution's plans related to major goals, executive management and responsible officers and committees as required for validation against their objectives. Accountability for external scrutiny is also facilitated by an integrated planning and review cycle. An example is provided in Figure 4.2, which illustrates the external and internal reporting requirements in an Australian university. Similar external and internal budgetry and quality reporting mechanisms are relevant in other countries.

To ensure high-quality reviews of their programmes by operational units such as schools and administrative departments, and of their strategic plans in accordance with current strategic directions, there should be:

1 An agreed schedule of reviews.
2 Review and planning policies.
3 An agreed model.
4 Congruence between performance indicators used for these reviews, annual reviews and planning activities.
5 The possibility of aligning professional accreditation processes with programme review and planning processes.

A model for review and planning should be developed by a working party of representatives from a range of operational units, and the institution's academic board, council or similar body. The model should be widely circulated for discussion throughout the institution.

A model for programme and planning review

A typical model for programme and planning review using a five-phase process of implementation is presented. It incorporates the following five critical elements:

1 Management of programmes.
2 Operational unit autonomy in decision-making.
3 Operational unit review of processes and its strategic plan.
4 Clear identification of roles and procedures for the conduct of reviews.
5 A quality assurance system as a basis for sustained and continuous improvement.

Stage 1: Planning and organizing the process

The operational unit, with assistance from personnel responsible for quality improvement across the institution, should:

1 Absorb the institution's policy on programme and planning review and become familiar with the resources provided to assist the process.
2 Clarify the focus of the review and develop a plan for the conduct of the process.

3 Select a review management team and coordinator from among the staff.
4 Identify the roles and responsibilities of the review management team and coordinator, other staff and the institution's quality improvement personnel.
5 Ensure appropriate student and community representatives are involved throughout.
6 Select and invite one or more external validator(s).
7 Commence building the operational unit profile. This should include:
   • vision, mission and value statements;
   • recent annual reports and reviews;
   • operational unit policies and procedures manual;
   • descriptions of available services;
   • results and analyses of surveys;
   • staff list and profiles;
   • details of management structures.

Stage 2: Self-assessment

The operational unit staff should undertake a self-assessment in accordance with guidelines and manuals for the programme and planning review process and procedures. The self-assessment steps should include:

1 Ensuring staff have a clear understanding of any criteria statements, and familiarity with the institution's vision, mission, values, goal statements and strategic plans.
2 Reviewing any examples of indicators of evidence for each of the criterion statements, and developing their own indicators where necessary.
3 Listing evidence which reflects the reality of the operational unit's situation.
4 Determining staff satisfaction levels with the degree to which each of the criteria has been met by the unit, based on the identified evidence.
5 Listing areas of strength and areas in need of change with respect to each of the criterion statements.

Stage 3: Reviewing the strategic plan

The steps for this stage should include:

1 Reviewing the list of strengths and areas in need of change and placing them into one of the following four categories:

- well established strengths which are important to maintain;
- strengths that are not so well established and need continual support;
- areas needing change that can be addressed easily;
- areas needing change that will require greater time and effort.

2 Revising the current strategic plan in the light of selected priority elements. The plan should:
- sustain and extend the strengths;
- address the areas needing change;
- be student-focused;
- provide opportunities for the greatest involvement of all key education partners;
- give full consideration to the external environment and its importance in providing opportunities and creating threats to the operational unit.

3 Making certain there is provision in the strategic plan for the direct involvement of the operational unit's constituents, such as stakeholders from the rest of the institution, staff, students and the wider community, in enhancing student services, research activities, research support, client services, staff development and community services.

4 Reviewing the operational unit's mission statement in light of the revised strategic plan – the strategic plan should be discussed with the immediate superior (e.g. faculty dean, divisional director or pro vice-chancellor).

Stage 4: Validation of the review

External validation is an integral component of a review process. The primary task of the external validator(s) is to provide an outside and unbiased perspective. The validator(s) should:

1 Agree or disagree with the staff satisfaction rating for each of the criteria.

2 Validate the operational unit's vision, mission and value statements for appropriateness in the light of its objectives and the goals of the institution.

3 Review the operational unit's summary of strengths and areas needing change, and note matters that may not have been identified by the staff.

4 Respond to the operational unit's strategic plan and determine its appropriateness.

5 Respond to the appropriateness of directions and targets in the strategic plan.

6 Meet with the staff, students and community representatives (where appropriate) and, from their perspective, discuss the strengths, areas needing change and the appropriateness of the strategic plan.
7 Complete a written report including recommendations regarding the operational procedures within the unit.

Stage 5: Accountability and implementation

The operational unit staff should:

1 Analyse and consolidate the results of the self-assessment and external validation reports.
2 Consolidate the strategic plan for the next five or six years and identify performance indicators.
3 Submit the strategic plan to the immediate superior, who subsequently will provide the executive and relevant institutional board or committee with the following information:
   • details of the operational unit, date of the review and the list of members involved in the review;
   • a brief report stating that the procedures for the review have been complied with, indicating any unresolved issues or significant matters that have been considered.

The flowchart in Figure 4.3 illustrates a model for the reporting procedures for the completed programme and planning review process.
   In developing policy on monitoring and review, it is important to include an outline of the procedures, with a schedule of responsibility for each of the following:

• annual reviews;
• five- or six-yearly programme and planning reviews;
• course reviews.

A model for course reviews

A model for course reviews is presented. Its articulation with five- or six-yearly programme and planning reviews, as well as an annual review of performance and progress to targets, is included. The following actions should be taken:

1 Embed a reference to course review in other review processes (for example, in programme and planning reviews' self-assessment

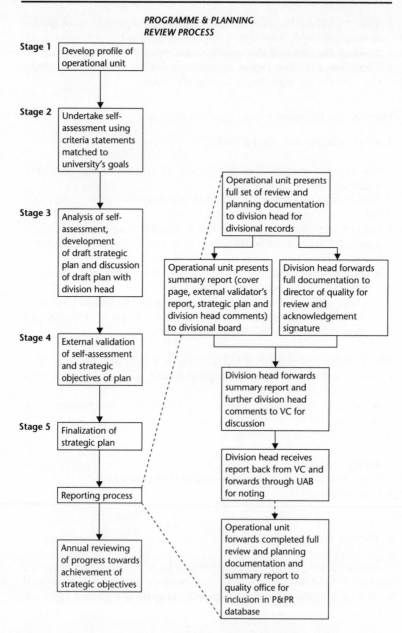

Figure 4.3 Flowchart of programme and planning review.

criteria, requesting a summation of the school's or department's course review management, seeking progress on targets for course reviews in annual review).
2 Identify basic principles and procedures for conducting course reviews.

Procedures for review of courses

1 Determine timing: for example, five- or six-yearly cycle of course reviews with clearly identified schedule (not to coincide with a full programme and planning review year).
2 Administration: reviews should be administered and serviced by the faculty, school or department, with support as appropriate from the central institutional administration.
3 Identify related committees:
- school or department level, e.g. course review committee, advisory committees and boards (*self-review and peer review function*);
- faculty or divisional level, e.g. faculty or divisional academic boards (*reporting function*);
- institution level, e.g. institutional academic board, teaching and learning committees, courses committees (*approval and process monitoring function*).

Structure of the Review (four stages)

1 *Preparation*. Gathering data and information (where appropriate from an executive information system).
2 *The review*. (a) Preparation of report based on a course review template. (b) Submission of report to relevant committees.
3 *Implementation of review outcomes*. Implementation should be the responsibility of the dean and head of school or department in accordance with the policies and processes of the institution. The head of school or department should also take appropriate action. Target dates for particular implementation measures should be set, in consultation with the dean and head of school or department.
4 *Follow-up procedures*. Review of implementation. Course coordinator or head of school to report to the dean, deputy vice-chancellor or vice-president on progress with recommendations after one year.

When one is using the following template there should be a focus on ensuring that evidence for each of the criteria is available, and that they can be evaluated and measured.

Courses review template

1 Course description.

2 Course details:
   • title;
   • name of school teaching the course;
   • name and contact details of course coordinator;
   • year in which the course was first offered.

3 Course review history:
   • years in which the course has been reviewed;
   • results of previous review(s);
   • major or minor changes made to the course since last course review.

4 Impact of any course changes.

5 Course objectives.

6 Aim of the course:
   • what is the purpose of the course?
   • how does it assimilate with the school's or department's teaching programme?
   • how does it help to achieve objectives?

7 Specific course objectives and outcomes:
   • what are the learning objectives of the course?
   • how do they integrate the teaching and learning objectives?
   • how do they relate to the research and development plan?
   • are these outcomes relevant, measurable and achievable?
   • is the course meeting these objectives?

8 School and interdepartmental links:
   • how does the course relate to other courses that the school or department offers?
   • how does it relate to courses run by other schools or departments?
   • is there a high degree of similarity with other courses being offered?
   • is there a method of integrating similar courses being offered by different schools or departments?

9 Links to institution and school or department strategic goals and values:
   • how does the course embody the institution's values?
   • does the course integrate the school's or department's and institution's strategic directions and goals? If so, how? If not, why not?

10 Links to the external community:
- how does the course relate to similar courses at other institutions?
- is the course being benchmarked against courses offered nationally or internationally? If so, how does the course compare?
- has the course content been reviewed in terms of compatibility with national and international industry trends in the discipline?
- how has the course been modified in response to disciplinary trends?

11 Course structure. How is the course structured, in terms of:
- tertiary entry requirements;
- duration of the course;
- credit points;
- number of hours per week;
- advanced standing where appropriate?

Is the structure of the course appropriate to achieving the learning objectives of the course?

12 Teaching delivery:
- how is the course delivered: (a) lectures, tutorials, practical sessions or laboratories, Internet, computer-assisted learning packages; (b) full-time, part-time, offshore or transnationally; (c) external study, videoconferencing etc.?
- does this delivery style suit the structure of the course?
- does the delivery style meet the needs of students, graduates and teaching staff?
- what student and graduate feedback is there to support this (for example, student and graduate survey results)?
- what is the format of course assessment?
- how does this assessment relate to the learning objectives?
- is the course assessment appropriate?
- is there any feedback from students regarding course assessment?
- if the students deem the assessment to be inappropriate, what improvements, if any, should be made?

13 Student intake and progress:
- what is the annual student enrolment rate?
- have there been any trends in the demand for the course?
- what are the attrition rates?
- what is the course completion rate?

14 Student profile:
- are students mainly full-time or part-time?
- are they fee-paying, overseas, external?
- is there a mix of postgraduate and undergraduate students?

15 Needs of the student group in terms of equal opportunity and support:
- are there any specific student needs (such as building access, cross-cultural awareness, language) that should be catered for?
- in what way are these student needs being met?

16 Resources and support for course:
- what is the staff profile?
- what is the student to staff ratio?
- how many teaching and supervision hours do staff complete?
- what is the level of staff qualifications and experience?
- how many sessional academics are employed as lecturers or tutors?
- do sufficient staffing levels exist to meet the learning objectives and support the assessment framework?
- how many staff have teaching qualifications?
- what is the ratio of full-time to part-time staff; tenured to non-tenured staff?

17 Course resources:
- are there updated library references available for the students (books, handouts, notes available on closed reserve)?
- is there sufficient access to information (web, frequency of tutorials, conferring hours of academic staff)?
- is there appropriate access to computer facilities and software?
- do students need remote access to course materials, and is it provided?
- are there sufficient physical resources in terms of lecture theatres and laboratory spaces?

18 Course costing:
- what is the expenditure per effective full-time student unit (EFTSU) or similar?
- what is the teaching and learning expenditure per successful EFTSU?
- does the course attract full fee-paying students?
- is the course financially viable?
- is there budget allowed for future course development?

19 Course feedback and review.
   (a) Professional accreditation (if applicable):
   - is the course subject to regular reviews from professional bodies?
   - what were the outcomes of these reviews?
   - is the course currently accredited; by whom?

(b) Advisory committee and board of study:
  - is feedback sought from these groups?
  - how is the feedback used?

20 Graduate outcomes:
  - is the employability of graduates reviewed, using graduate destination surveys?
  - is there contact with employer groups (e.g. knowledge of potential employer groups, representation on advisory committees and boards)?
  - how many recent graduates are in full-time employment in the six months after completing their degree; what are their earnings levels?
  - how does this compare with similar courses offered at other institutions?

21 Industry feedback:
  - are employers provided with the opportunity to provide feedback on the quality of the course and graduates?
  - is a graduate attributes survey used to gauge employer feedback?
  - how satisfied are employer groups with graduates from the course, and with the course itself?

22 Recommendations of the courses review committee and their implications:
  - is the course viable?
  - what are the particular strengths of the course?
  - are there any matters that might need to be addressed?
  - are there any key recommendations?
  - what are the resource (human, physical, financial) implications of these recommendations?
  - what impact will the recommendations have on academic support (e.g. library, academic registry office, careers office, marketing and international programmes, counselling)?
  - what actions must be taken (e.g. changes to the calendar or handbook)?

The preceding examples of processes which may be used to monitor improvement of quality in post-secondary education environments have been presented in detail. They have been derived from common features of review processes in institutions in a range of countries, and from literature on the topic.

Tools

Around one-third of the *Business Review Weekly*/American Express Top 500 companies use the tools of quality management.[5] There are a number of quality management tools which are primarily used for problem-solving, including:

- *Pareto analysis.* A vertical bar chart is created to display the number of occurrences of errors or problems on the horizontal line, and their frequency by type on the vertical line, over a set period of time. A meaningful unit of measure is chosen (for example, frequency or cost), and problems to be monitored or compared are rank ordered by brainstorming or use of existing data. They can be used to help to focus on causes that will have the greatest impact. Based on the Pareto principle that 20 per cent of the sources cause 80 per cent of the problem, the charts can have a number of variations: for example, *before and after* to show the effect of change; *source of data* where a number of charts show data from different departments, locations, programmes and so on.
- *Cause and effect diagram.* The fishbone diagram (as it is called because of its appearance) was first introduced by Ishikawa. It displays all the possible causes related to a problem or condition, in increasing detail, to discover its root cause. The snapshot of relationships focuses on finding and curing causes, rather than on addressing the symptoms. The major causes are connected by lines (bones) to the backbone line, which has an arrow pointing to the effect (What? Where? When? How much?). Categories explored should be equipment, people, materials and methods. In response to questions relating to each of the categories, possible causes are placed along each of the major cause bones. Solutions are more evident where causes appear repeatedly.
- *Checksheets.* Structured documents designed to record and compile data from a particular event. Trends and patterns can be detected over time.
- *Control charts, histograms, scattergrams.* Used to collect common versus special causes in variation in process performance over time, control charts are run charts with calculated control limits. Histograms can be used to show the number of occurrences of a given variable over a specific time. The frequency distribution is graphically presented in bar form. A scattergram is the graphical representation of two variables (e.g. light or temperature, and speed of production or quality of product), and their relationship to each other.

There are many other tools that can be utilized, including activity network diagrams (such as Gantt charts), affinity diagrams, brainstorming, experiments, flowcharts, force fields, interrelationship diagraphs, matrices, multivariate analysis, nominal group technique, operations research, prioritization, process capability, radar charts, sampling, sensory tests, statistical methods, storyboards, ranking, stratification and tree diagrams. It is beyond the scope of this text to present these in detail. Information on their applicability in specific situations, diagrams and information on how quality management tools can be used to make the most of data and knowledge of staff to improve decision-making for continuous improvement can be found in a number of books.[6]

Measurement

Organizations which apply quality management principles and practices use data and information widely and wisely. Key performance measures for processes and outcomes are identified and measured. Statistical and charting techniques identified in the preceding section on tools are used at all levels for decision-making and reporting. Decisions are made on sound evidence, not gut reactions. Actions are based on knowledge and understanding, together with sensible and sensitive application of measurement – in context – and with an acceptance of the value of diversity.

The desired outcome determines which measures are used. It is argued that the outcomes in post-secondary education are difficult to measure. The processes involved in delivering products (e.g. teaching courses and undertaking research) pose special dilemmas in measurement methodology.

It seems relevant to the earlier basis of accreditation in standard setting, and an evolution to address qualitative as well as quantitative measures or outcomes, to remind ourselves that the behavioural objectives movement reached a high point in the 1950s to 1970s with the publication of a trilogy of taxonomic texts. Bloom *et al.* (1956) sought to classify educational standards by identifying a range of goals or objectives in the cognitive area.[7] Measurement of outcomes may be applied to such activities as thinking, remembering, problem-solving, recalling, knowing and creating. The use of such a taxonomy provides a hierarchy of categories which should be considered in relation to educational objectives. A variety of items may be used to assess the standard achieved in each of the objectives. The standard may be considered *higher order* when *understanding, translating and interpreting* are involved. The use of a hierarchical model for the taxonomy allows for a flowchart of objectives as they relate to one another.

As well as the cognitive domain which deals more with knowledge acquisition and the development of intellectual abilities and skills, both the affective and psychomotor domains were addressed by Bloom and his associates.[8] The taxonomy produced was intentionally neutral, and a descriptive representation of the range of intended behaviours indicated from the range of educational goals, objectives, curricula, instructional information and methods.

At the outset, it was established that efforts to measure performance should be focused on the clients – the graduates. End-of-course evaluations do not assist those students who have problems along the way. A range of measures to consider student opinions on the course, services, facilities, teaching and learning experiences, as well as their satisfaction level compared with what they would judge as ideal, are useful. These, linked to surveys of students who exit before successful completion, graduates, employers and alumni over time, have been identified as more valuable measures of processes, products and outcomes: that is, the inputs, throughputs and outputs.[9]

The next section, on evaluation, provides a historical perspective through a review of the literature on the evolution of models, and further evidence of the range of methods used to measure performance in post-secondary education.

Evaluation

Historical overview

Although the term *educational evaluation* was not seen to have been used formally until it was coined by R. Tyler in the 1930s, there were moves to introduce standardized testing by Howe and Mann in the 1840s, while Rice established comparative research techniques to determine student achievements between 1887 and 1898.[10] Meanwhile, a push to evaluate secondary schools, to assist informed student admission, commenced at the University of Michigan,[11] and was followed by the formation of the North Central Association of Schools and Colleges in 1902, which developed a form of accreditation for secondary schools in 1905 as previously indicated.

Tyler's approach involved the need to evaluate how well a programme met its objectives, and others followed his model of *goal attainment*, which was influential because of its clarity in developing easily measurable criteria.[12] The criticisms of this method included those of Suchman (once one of its strongest advocates), who highlighted the difficulty of measuring a multiplicity of complex and overlapping objectives.[13] Wolf saw the need to seek the views of the stakeholders in the programmes, and recognized the importance of looking at side-effects in general, including negative or other outcomes, which were not among those criteria measured.[14] Robinson expressed concerns that where there were broad aims, it was difficult to see the outcomes or goals, and there was a risk of inhibiting flexibility and innovation in programmes.[15] That the stakeholders may wish to ascribe different goals independently to a programme with broad aims was yet another difficulty associated with the goal-attainment approach.

In the 1960s, the course of education evaluation was changed by the directions taken by Cronbach, who believed that evaluation should serve to improve the education process, and by Stufflebeam, Scriven and Stake.[16] In different ways they all envisaged moving to a holistic and complete evaluation of the complexity of programmes, their context and the range of outcomes. Furthermore, they saw the importance of judging the value or merit of each programme. The evaluation model that evolved was *decision-oriented*, as espoused by Stufflebeam and colleagues; or *consumer-oriented*, as perceived by Scriven, who rejected the views of Tyler (for not incorporating a judgemental role) and Cronbach (for concentrating on *formative* evaluation), and promoted the concept of a *goal-free, summative* evaluation model.[17]

It was Stake who emphasized the value of client-centred evaluation. In a number of papers, he at first embraced Tyler's objectives orientation, but later moved to what he termed *responsive evaluation*.[18] The enlightenment which followed, which was a feature of this model, was seized as a concept by Partlett and his colleagues when they coined the term *illuminative evaluation*.[19] Kemmis was another who saw the value of attending to the views (responses) of the stakeholders in the evaluation process, especially as they relate to the critical debate which these views may stimulate, and through which the programme is illuminated.[20] More recently, evaluation methods have been developed in an attempt to operationalize the assumptions about, and theories of, organizational learning. Sharp has devised a goal attainment scaling (GAS) methodology for evaluating organizational learning in terms of a change in organizational culture, and a change in the acquisition of knowledge.[21] Thus there is seen to be a range of approaches or models of evaluation which overlap in many instances.[22]

Uses of evaluation

In a discussion of evaluation, Stufflebeam and Shinkfield suggest three main uses: (a) for accountability purposes; (b) to provide enlightenment; and (c) to foster improvement.[23] By providing information about a current programme through self-study reporting, with external confirmation and clarification, there may be improvement (or maintenance) in the quality of the programme. Accountability may be achieved through providing written evidence as feedback to interested parties about the programme and its outcomes or products. *Enlightenment* is a comfortable and comforting term where judgement and other subjective approaches are used instead of the research or investigative model.[24] Furthermore, Stake proposes the equation that evaluation is equal to the whole constellation of values for any programme, divided by the complexities in criteria and expectations of the stakeholders:[25] that is, an observed value is compared with some standard.

Stufflebeam and his colleagues have defined evaluation as the process of delineating, obtaining and providing useful information for judging decision alternatives.[26] So evaluation is *delineating* (defining and specifying what will be assessed in the programme, institution and the like), *obtaining* (collecting, organizing and analysing the information) and *providing* (synthesizing the information for decision-makers). It is historically interesting to note that as early as the 1950s, the emphasis for some decision-makers in evaluation had moved from focusing on the *process* to focusing on the *outcomes*.[27]

The debate on evaluation in post-secondary education is aligned better to a softer approach to considering the quality of outcomes. A sensitive approach to quality management supports a somewhat loose hierarchy of high-level standards, improvement targets and performance indicators, the inclusiveness and continuity of stakeholder opinion in their development and application and the subtleties of interpretation biased towards improvement rather than control. The high-level standards approach comes in various guises, and has moved to include the development and adoption of citizens' or students' charters.

It is from the background of standard setting, identification of objectives and their relationship to evaluation that the process of accreditation and audits may be seen to forge ahead with an increasing volume of paperwork being expected from the group or institution being accredited or audited. Despite all this activity, and while there is a theoretical basis established for methods used in evaluation, it appears that there is, to this point, no commonly accepted theory of educational accreditation or quality audit.

Costs and casualties ▌

Florida Power and Light became famous by winning Japan's coveted Deming Prize in 1989. Having done so, it had to review the results and revise its way of doing business quickly, before many of the rigidly applied quality techniques it had implemented, to win the prize, assured its demise.[28] The story is a familiar one for many companies which are used as examples by those espousing the philosophies of the new managerialism. Peters and Waterman cite many of them in *A Search For Excellence*, and some of the subnational public sector organizations in the USA are presented by Osborne and Gaebler in *Reinventing Government*.[29] These revelations provide a portent for those who chase quality awards or accreditation as the prize, instead of a cultural and organizational change that is clearly focused on delivering superior value which is beneficial to all.

Many Western governments are now insisting that their suppliers have, or need to be seeking, an acceptable form of quality certification as a prerequisite to delivering a product or service. However, organizations must be careful not to install compliance with standards, like the ISO 9000 series, as their mission.[30] Such compliance is but one means, albeit laudable, towards the end of continually improving beneficiary value. Measurement and attention to processes must support and not overpower the client focus of adding value and benefit while engaging service strategies. The outcomes are the focus, not the processes by which they are achieved.

However, equally dangerous is the adoption of, and strict adherence to, simple-minded client service standards. Aspects of service that may be readily quantified and analysed, such as waiting times, number of students enrolled, complaints filed, cycle times for answering correspondence, approvals registered on questionnaires and the like, might make managers feel comfortable about their organization's or education institution's customer or client service effort. They do not provide a means for creating value for those who are receiving the product or service. Post-secondary education institutions, in particular, should not be in the business of treating clients like statistics: for example, focusing on who is supposed to be measuring whom and for what purpose.

Client research might have revealed that waiting time was not an issue, but rather the perception that the institution's processes and people are wasting the clients' time. Using a true client focus approach involves the implementation of service strategies which would ensure that clients perceive that their time is being used productively. This might involve education programmes and/or alternative access initiatives for some clients whose needs can be met without them having to attend at all.[31] There is a strong likelihood that measuring and improving the effectiveness of these strategies will reduce waiting times all round.

This brief discussion serves to highlight some ways of implementing quality service thinking, and also highlights the dysfunction of the single-minded pursuit of simple-minded standards. However, evidence of high failure rates among organizations that have implemented TQM continues to mount, especially in those that are highly bureaucratic or are in the service industries.[32] Partly, this could be a function of the temporal differences between TQM and quality service or service success models, or it might stem from a poor interpretation of the concepts, or a lack of commitment to see them through. Does this mean that the post-secondary education sector should not use new concepts, or concepts from business and industry, because the sector won't do it right? What would have actually failed: the concept or the way it was operationalized? More information on quality service models can be found in Chapter 7.

Making the client feel better should not be at the expense of forgetting about having more satisfying and stimulating work for staff at all levels. A dilemma could arise if the education institution lost sight of the importance of a comfortable internal climate for staff in affording undue primacy to the expectations of external clients. James Strong, the chief executive officer of Qantas, recently had to redress such an imbalance by appealing to passengers, via the airline's inflight magazine *The Australian Way*, to exhibit more tolerance for his employees' efforts in aspiring to exemplary levels of service. He asked passengers to notice and commend good service and not berate staff when they failed to meet exemplary standards.[33]

A recent survey of 300 large Australian companies, conducted by the Centre for Corporate Change at the University of New South Wales, found that the main reason for TQM programmes failing is that individuals and management lack commitment to them: people simply do not want to be empowered.[34] Morgan and Murgatroyd develop this argument further by introducing the concept of *contrapreneurship*, which is described as effectively and creatively using skills and competencies to prevent the occurrence of significant change.[35] These authors suggest that contrapreneurship is much more difficult to counter than passive resistance, cynicism or simple human inertia.

There is an assertion, which originated with W. Edwards Deming, who spoke of a *chain reaction*, that quality costs less.[36] It is claimed that cost improvements can be achieved because some less than satisfactory processes, such as poor procedures and duplication of effort, can be found and eliminated through what is termed *process re-engineering.*[37] This may be true initially in areas where processes are simply adhered to because of some historical precedence, and were either poorly engineered in the first place or have subsequently been integrated by layers rather than re-engineered. Even so, empowering staff to find them involves an increase in their time commitment, which might be freely obtained through some sort of *Hawthorne effect*, or might not.[38] It could be argued that such desirable staff behaviour should be positively reinforced through some reward or recognition system, particularly early in the cultural transformation necessary to bring about change. The available evidence from successful organizations suggests that this transformation takes five or more years. Cycle time reduction is presented in Chapter 7 as a model for re-engineering.

Another element which should be considered is whether the initial gains are discounted in the future when the latent rationale for some discarded procedures re-emerges. Perhaps there is truth in the adage that can be applied here: don't throw the baby out with the bath water. Furthermore, the possibility of increasing costs initially should not be discounted. It may be necessary to spend more on quality-related initiatives at the outset to gain more sustainable improvement, with less risk, at some time in the future.[39]

Pondering the costs and casualties of quality improvement strategies should clarify the issue that care must be taken to ensure that the measurements don't overpower the strategies. It should be recognized that new management approaches and other reforms require both political vision and space to allow them to work.[40]

Chapter 5 focuses on the importance of linking quality management to planning, so that they become the foundation and framework for all activities undertaken in post-secondary education institutions.

5

LINKING QUALITY MANAGEMENT TO PLANNING

Introduction

In Chapter 4, practical examples of the application of quality management processes and practices to the post-secondary education sector were presented. Without close links to planning, quality management is unsuccessful. Building quality management strategies into all levels of planning facilitates acceptance of, adaptation to and comfort with regular reviews to monitor improvement.

This chapter affirms that planning begins with identifying and setting strategic directions to guide advancement to best practice as determined by each institution. A framework is suggested. Steps in scenario planning are given, as well as information about hierarchical and other structures in organizations. Workforce planning is used as an example of how quality management is linked to planning at the corporate and functional unit level.

Setting strategic directions

A strategic directions process includes:

1 Identifying key environmental and stakeholder considerations, including management of risk.
2 Scenario planning; reviewing the organization's vision, mission, core products and services, values and goals.
3 Reviewing (identifying, defining) strategic objectives and prioritizing them.
4 Defining associated key performance indicators.

It is also important to define factors critical to the organization's success (that is, the achievement of strategic objectives) and the attainment of competitive advantage.

A framework for strategic initiatives

To address the key elements of a strategic directions approach, a framework (in the context of critical success factors) and associated strategic initiatives can be developed to progress the education institution.

At the outset it is important to understand the stakeholders:

1 Those who influence the institution (governments, legislators, business and industry associations, agencies, competitors, unions, insurers, taxpayers, alumni, research granting bodies, private investors).
2 Those who work in the institution (academic and general staff, sessional and contract staff, researchers, consultants, visiting fellows).
3 Those who are impacted by the institution and its products (e.g. courses) and services (students, parents, employers, employees, industry and commerce, national and international communities, the political system, other education institutions, society, all other stakeholders).

The next element in the framework is identifying the core business for the future. The measures of success should be in terms of:

1 Products and services (e.g. undergraduate and postgraduate degree courses, research, continuing education, all at local, national and international levels; consultancy services; open and flexible delivery and multimedia modes).
2 Direction (e.g. reducing or increasing the number of courses, growth opportunities for local or international students and offshore course delivery).
3 Outputs (e.g. graduates, ideas and innovations, increase in knowledge and skill levels).
4 Who benefits (e.g. graduates, employers, community, society, staff, the institution).

Evidence of success should be sought, and to this end, a service success model could be used. A model of service quality for success is presented in Chapter 7.

Key questions to ask in setting directions

There are a number of key questions that should be considered when planning the future. Until these are answered, scenario planning is difficult. They include:

- Who will we serve?
- Through what channels will we reach clients?
- What image do we want to project in the market place?
- What will be the nature of our business in the future?
- Who or what will be our competitors?
- On what will we base competitive advantage?
- What capabilities, courses, research programmes will make us unique?
- How will we organize and manage our resources, including the workforce?

For the post-secondary education sector, a set of possible response topics is presented as they relate to three major questions. The questions and responses should be deliberated in the light of external drivers in the environment, and each institution's values.

1 *Question*: What will we be doing? *Answer*: Advancing and transferring knowledge; providing relevant courses.
2 *Question*: What do we want to achieve? *Answer*: Outcomes related to strategic objectives; realize our vision.
3 *Question*: How will we do it? *Answer*: Via strategic initiatives related to critical success factors; by monitoring performance against key performance indicators and managing risk; by using core processes of teaching, learning and research; through marketing.

Scenario planning

When the organization has established a broad base of strategic intelligence and has a continuous scanning and monitoring system, scenario planning works well. Taking into account a range of environmental factors – social dynamics, economic issues, political issues and technological issues – a number of questions can be asked about the forces and factors (internal and external) which can manipulate the future in different directions.

By constructing stories about the future – plausible, alternative and structurally different views, not predictions or snapshots, which are *forecasting* the future – a range of scenarios can be created. Each scenario should be plausible and distinct, and provide a framework for structuring perceptions about alternative future environments. Not identifying the right or critical uncertainties, and the time required to construct the scenarios, may be seen to be disadvantageous.

The steps in scenario-based planning are:

- determining the strategic decision to be illuminated;
- identifying the things to be clear when making the decision;
- assessing the environmental drivers and forces;
- elaborating (graphically and in detail) on selected scenarios;
- interpreting the scenarios through considering the opportunities and threats and the options available – that is, rethinking the future.

When one is setting directions, after considering scenarios, the structure of the organization should be considered.

Deciding on the optimum structure

Institutions may have a vertical hierarchy of divisional and departmental management; a process structure where there are no divisions or departments as such; or a combination of these two. Most education institutions have a combined structure, but some may have a traditional vertical hierarchy. These are sometimes termed functional organizations, and are characterized as being:

1 Stable and predictable.
2 Based on functional competencies (focused, with a narrow knowledge and skill base).
3 High in the degree of staff specialization.
4 Narrow in the scope of work (teaching, research, accounting, gardening).

The strength of the vertical structure is its simple, efficient system, where limited knowledge and skills are needed by each employee, and in which technical competencies and knowledge domains are reinforced. Weaknesses include limited flexibility, difficulty in transferring knowledge across functions and few incentives for organization-wide integration. By overlaying the traditional hierarchical structure with processes across the organization, more than one focus can be achieved. Weaknesses lie in multiple reporting relationships (e.g. for teaching and research staff), inefficient coordination and incompatibility with traditional styles of management. However, the strengths should not be ignored. They include flexibility, responsiveness and improved resource utilization.

Once scenarios have been considered, the structure affirmed or revised and the directions set, specific strategies for each operational plan must be considered.

Strategy setting in planning

One of the key enabling processes in redesigning the organization is workforce planning and staff development at all levels. Leaders and managers require training and development as much as any other member of the workforce. In order to provide an example of how planning is linked to quality management, workforce planning, as it articulates with staff training and development, is presented.

Workforce planning

There are four major elements of workforce planning:

1 Investigation (analysis of the institution's present position and workforce audit data).
2 Forecasting (future estimates of outputs and staff capabilities' requirements).
3 Planning and goal-setting (to progress from the present position to the forecast scenario).
4 Control (ongoing monitoring and evaluation of timely goal achievement on budget).

Investigation

Before deciding how to improve the workforce position, it is important to review the current status. To assess this, key data must be collected and statistically aggregated. They should include an analysis of the numbers of people (academic and general) employed by:

- level;
- job or position;
- gender (to be used judiciously);
- age (to be used judiciously);
- length of service;
- skill or education level (qualifications);
- competencies and other requirements relevant to the level.

It is also necessary to find out how the workforce is being used (e.g. turnover, absenteeism, productivity), then to analyse each factor in turn. Collating this information should form the basis for a comprehensive and coordinated staff development system being aware of current capabilities of employees, immediate and future needs for the workforce and how they link to planning and budgeting for staff development programmes.

Forecasting

Workforce planning involves working with the institution's corporate and divisional, faculty, departmental and school strategic plans to predict workforce requirements. By examining the plans and a range of scenarios for the future, a decision can be made about how many and what kinds of staff are needed. This is a matter of using techniques to forecast supply and demand. Whatever forecasting technique is used, there are likely to be gaps and shortfalls. To predict which gaps might occur, it is necessary to decide how, or if, staff shortages in a particular skill area will affect the institution's future success, and whether the gap between supply and demand decreases or increases over time.

Planning and control

These two topics cannot be dealt with in isolation. They are intricately linked. After determination of whether the future promises labour shortages or surpluses, strategies can be put in place. Once the workforce needs have been identified and strategies agreed, implementation should take place. The link between personnel management (especially recruitment and selection), a training and development system, and corporate strategic planning is critical for an institution's ultimate success through competitive advantage.

Workforce planning is a continuous process of constant evaluations and adjustments, with direct links to other personnel management functions, corporate planning (the organization's overall business plan) and strategic planning (the long-range business plan based on environmental change and organizational capability in new areas).

Personnel management

The management of personnel is a core activity and can no longer be relegated to human resource staff as a stand-alone human resource

Table 5.1 Workforce planning links

Workforce planning	Corporate planning	Strategic planning
Recruitment and selection (position descriptions)	Resources (including human resources)	All matters including human resources
Training and development	Technology	must be assessed to
Performance assessment	Financial position	inform the strategic
Performance management	Production performance and market position	planning process as a prelude to operational plans
Identifying potential	Economic trends	
Promotions; transfers	Legislation	
Career and succession management	Actions of competitors	
Wages; salary administration	Government policy	
Remuneration and benefits	Social trends	
Productivity		
Records and statistics		
Job design		
Cost control		
Personnel information systems		

or personnel management issue.[1] It must be addressed in the context of overall strategic planning linked to budget, performance and outcomes, as illustrated in Table 5.1. In addition, and simply represented, Figure 5.1 shows the linkages between workforce planning, training and development and personnel management as vital elements of an institution's management procedures.

Ongoing monitoring, evaluation and review of all components of personnel management, staff development and planning is necessary to ensure continuous improvement (exceeding goals and clients' expectations). Figure 5.2 shows how the training and development cycle can be linked to personnel management and workforce planning through information gained from performance appraisals and job specification in position descriptions.

It is clear from Figure 5.2 that workforce planning is driven by organizational strategies which can be developed after using a tool such as scenario planning to ask questions about the future. Advantages gained from using scenario planning include the development of ongoing and long-term strategy-focused thinking and learning. Thereby the organization will be able to see the need to develop the knowledge and skills of all staff to prepare for the future.

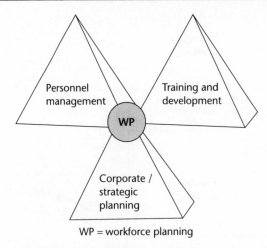

WP = workforce planning

Figure 5.1 Links between workforce planning, personnel management, training and development, and corporate/strategic planning.

Components of personnel management

A key element of planning is the management of people in the organization. There are a number of components of personnel management which have been identified in the workforce planning links (Table 5.1). These include position descriptions, training and development and performance assessment and management.

Position descriptions (PDs)

The process of job specification (recorded as a PD) follows these steps:

- job analysis;
- job description selecting jobs which provide a benchmark;
- job evaluation;
- job grading;
- pay determination.

Unfortunately, job analysis is not simple. Jobs change, particularly in general staff positions, and therefore PDs must be updated yearly, so that future training and development programmes can be designed with relevance. Academic levels (e.g. tutors or associate lecturers, lecturers, assistant or associate professors and professors) should also have PDs which describe their range of responsibilities.

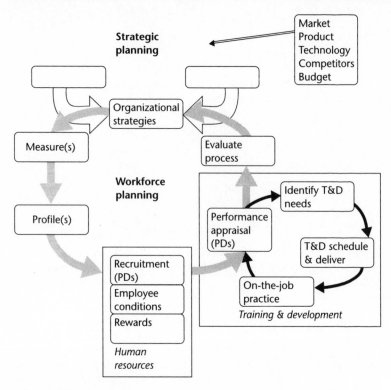

Figure 5.2 Links between workforce planning, personnel management, training and development, and corporate/division/ area strategic planning.

Job analysis consists of coming to terms with what the job actually entails. Breaking the job routine into daily, weekly, monthly and yearly tasks is a good method. Looking at those tasks which are triggered by outside events, such as a student enquiry about enrolling in a particular course in a flexible mode, will help to complete the detailed components of the job. Many tasks will not be triggered, but will be routine and predictable, such as maintenance or filing. Little by little, a detailed picture of the job is painted. From here the manager can see the kinds of skills necessary to perform the job.

To determine the gaps between the current capabilities of employees and recruitment or training and development needs, an important step is analysing the range of jobs undertaken in the area. To find out the demands of the job, the manager should conduct an analysis by:

- identifying the tasks;
- examining how, when and why they are performed;
- identifying the main duties and responsibilities;
- noting the job conditions.

From here a detailed PD may be created. Special considerations, such as performance standards and priorities, should be indicated in the PD in order to facilitate creation of *essential* and *desirable* criteria for recruitment and selection. Employees should participate in writing PDs and identifying essential and desirable selection criteria if possible.

Job evaluation begins by identifying differences among jobs, in terms of competencies required, and judging their relative value to the organization. In evaluation of jobs, two methods can be used: analytical and non-analytical. The first works by breaking jobs into parts and assigning points to each. The non-analytical method evaluates the jobs as a whole and ranks them according to other jobs. Hereafter, the grading or level determination and pay scale is established.

Training and development

Many people think training is something which only trainers do; or, worse still, something which can be done only in classes with lectures and textbooks. This is not the case. Training is not the same as education. The two activities differ in several ways.

Education is more focused on individuals' own growth and general enlightenment: that is, their further development. Education provides an opportunity for people to come into contact with a wide breadth of concepts, ideas and facts. Education ideally involves a lifelong learning ethic, whereas training can be short-term and for a specific task or job. Training is centred on providing a very specific set of skills, such as computer programming or selling. Training, therefore, tends to focus on the needs of the organization, but can also be readily linked to personal development and career advancement.

Effective training and development of the workforce is clearly linked to the economic development and productivity of a nation. In developing countries, the crucial factor for successful country or organizational progress is the extent to which local employees can acquire the necessary skills and pass them on to their colleagues, so training and development has several clear benefits to both individual and organization. It:

- speeds up learning time;
- increases efficiency and decreases waste (e.g. reduces student emigration);

- standardizes work;
- builds confidence;
- increases profit;
- decreases errors, mistakes and accidents.

Managers at every level of an organization, including post-secondary education institutions, should be actively involved in training and developing their people, even if they do not do it all themselves. Ultimately, managers, as much as individuals themselves, are responsible for employees' training and development. Some may be delegated to a staff development and training department, some to an outside training organization or higher education institution and some may be undertaken on the job. Whatever method is chosen, the manager remains responsible. This is because managers can properly assess employees' performance and progress, and determine, for all individuals, what kind of training and development they need and how they have responded to any received.

In order to achieve coordinated, highly effective and efficient staff development programmes, a good relationship between managers and the appropriate training and development department is critical. Managers should be able to rely on staff in the department to become familiar with external training agencies and sharpen their own training and development skills.

Checklist for staff development planning

The following checklist highlights the key areas on which managers must concentrate to prepare for their staff development responsibilities, and should be linked to elements of any policy and procedures. Consideration should be given to performance indicators, targets and measures for each element. Ideally the training and development system will provide a procedure for enabling the manager to:

- collaborate with the staff development department to determine staff training and experience needs;
- create priorities and a time-scale;
- cooperate on training courses by releasing staff and discussing the course with staff before and after creating a plan with them to put training and development arrangements into practice;
- carry out planned on-the-job training;
- occasionally instruct on courses to build and refresh skills.

Training and development planning should address the needs of the organization, not simply the education and development of the individual. It follows that the organization and the job should be examined first. In that way it is possible to identify those parts of the job where more training is needed; where there are problems (or faults, deviations or non-compliance) in the organization, and to isolate the situations where training and development can help.

Some issues to consider in formulating a staff development plan include:

- staff turnover rates, and retirement schedules;
- school-leavers, appropriate post-secondary graduates and local labour sources;
- legislation concerning those who may or must be employed (e.g. equal employment opportunity, or EEO, and diversity issues);
- changes in the organization's policy or products (e.g. courses);
- changes in working practices or standards (e.g. occupational health and safety, or OHS, environmental matters);
- equipment breakdowns;
- particular or repeated problems;
- new technology;
- new production sites, campuses and locations;
- what the competitors are doing;
- who else is competing for skilled labour (within or outside the post-secondary education sector).

Implementation, monitoring, evaluation and review are critical success factors for all planning. Analyses of needs are not the same as solutions. A staff development plan translates needs into action.

It is widely acknowledged that the rate at which knowledge is acquired, through current skill and knowledge development, is likely to be the only sustainable means of competitive advantage. Senge's concept of the learning organization – one which considers not only the development of knowledge, skills and attitudes but also the development of capacity to create and produce results – is the key to success.[2]

There are four options in managing training and development as they impact on the capabilities of the workforce.

- *Provision*: developing the best internal capability through on-the-job training and internally conducted courses.
- *Maintenance*: managing internal capability to meet costs and quality standards by continuing education in critical areas and reviewing training and development needs.
- *Brokering*: developing ongoing access to the best capability possible by scanning the internal and external environment and being

prepared to act as a consultant on availability of required and desired training and development opportunities.
- *Contracting out*: monitoring to ensure that this happens only for essential support work, including for training and development.

These options highlight the value of linking the assessment of training and development needs with performance management.

Performance management

The key characteristics of a structured system of staff development and performance management include:

- a clear definition of the attributes, knowledge and skills necessary to achieve business success;
- an understanding of the current attributes, knowledge and skills of the workforce;
- remuneration and reward mechanisms;
- individual acceptance of responsibility for learning in a timely manner linked to current and future business outcomes;
- a variety of learning mechanisms, with less emphasis on classroom training, and a focus on the evaluation and application of learning outcomes;
- personal and team performance contracts and agreements, and the use of self-assessment through to 360 degree feedback;
- quicker recognition and management of under-performance.

Performance management should be for everyone. A competency-based framework linking training and development, recruitment and selection, performance appraisal and career development is a useful foundation for improved institutional performance through the optimal performance and commitment of its workforce. The training and development needs of each area must be identified at least annually, and in an ongoing manner through formal and informal mechanisms.

Accountability measures to address performance indicators of efficiency and effectiveness should be established to ensure that training and development is value for money and actually to develop competence in those who participate. Translation of the knowledge and capabilities to the workplace (whether as a general or academic staff member, or as a manager, head or dean of a school) is even more important than freely providing staff development without monitoring its success.[3]

To ensure the effectiveness and efficiency of programmes and appropriate outcomes, evaluation of training and development should be made at the following stages:

1 Needs analysis.
2 Design.
3 Delivery.
4 Results.
5 Impact over time.

Each stage of the evaluation should have a *product,* which confirms that evaluation has occurred.

1 A needs analysis includes answering the following questions:
   • why do we need staff development?
   • who has the need?
   • what is the need?
   • what are the solutions?
   • what are the staff development objectives?
   Following this, the programme objectives should be established (this is the evaluation *product*).

2 Questions in the design stage include:
   • what is the best design or staff development programme alternative?
   • how should it be delivered?
   After *evaluating the alternatives* and the means to assure the quality of what is to be delivered, the programme design and implementation plan are the products.

3 At the delivery stage, the question is:
   • how was the programme delivered (organization, content, presentation, resources and the like)?
   This is *process evaluation*, and the product is improvement in programme delivery.

4 Results and impacts can be evaluated by looking subjectively and objectively at:
   • reaction from participants;
   • behavioural intention;
   • acquisition of knowledge and skills;
   • work behaviour (including in others);
   • institutional change (e.g. EEO initiatives, OHS initiatives, climate surveys);
   • impacts on performance (e.g. increased productivity, income, profit, client retention).

The *performance evaluation* product is being able to demonstrate the worth of the staff development programme.

Training and development can be incorporated as a system within the institutional structure if it forms part of the evaluation of institutional performance. A continuous loop should be established for staff development processes and procedures to provide a framework for a best practice staff development system:

Objectives → Inputs → Outputs → Outcomes → Impacts →

Evaluation → Criteria and Benchmarks → Performance →

With feedback to the objectives, the staff development cyclic system should be linked to overall institutional performance through the performance criteria and benchmarks stage.

By developing performance criteria based on benchmarks which link with strategic plans and taking account of clients' needs, as well as the institution's vision and short- and long-term goals, staff development can add value to the institution's performance and competitive advantage through a contemporary knowledge-based workforce.

Use of indicators

Performance indicators are used to demonstrate the extent to which operational units (such as schools and other academic as well as all general non-academic departments) are achieving desired results. Three dimensions of indicators must be considered contextually:

1 Appropriateness (directly relating to the core business and function of the institution).
2 Efficiency (monitored in terms of the actual use of resources given a fixed allocation, not simply the cost of individual functions). The aim is an improvement in performance against effectiveness indicators while using no more (and preferably less) than targeted resources: that is, performing better with less.
3 Effectiveness, considered the key to information about the quality of outcomes; the impact of what has been done, in the context of what the institution or operational unit has said will be done.

It should be noted that many published indicators are of workload. Workload indicators are about levels of inputs or activities, not performance.

The purpose of indicators

The key to quality improvement is a review of the sense of purpose and direction for each operational unit in the education institution. Operational units include general (e.g. human resources, finance) and academic (e.g. schools, departments, faculties) units. Each operational unit should be responsible for identifying its own *performance indicators*, *benchmarks* and *targets* to clarify the gap between current and desired practice.

These indicators, benchmarks and targets should be incorporated in strategic plans, reviewed and progressed regularly to operationalize the strategies. Plans should be living documents, not door-stops and bookshelf fillers. A plan on a page will do. It was the University of Queensland's David Warren Piper, in his *Quality Management in Universities, Volume 1,* who proposed that the reason why strategic planning is criticized for possibly stifling creativity and inhibiting flexibility is not the plans themselves but the way people use them. 'It can convincingly be claimed that once plans have been articulated and set down they are much more amenable to modification and to quick adjustment than plans which are tacit, or exist only in folklore and traditions of an organization.'[4]

Quantitative and qualitative indicators

Indicators are just that. They are signposts which indicate something about performance. Measures associated with indicators are both qualitative and quantitative. They can provide information on efficiency and effectiveness.

In post-secondary education, indicators can be used to look at the whole sector, by sector (vocational and higher education) or by institution. Reflecting on the sector as a whole will not affect institutional diversity, but will provide information about cost-effectiveness and general transparency. There has been little work on sector indicators by either private or public providers of post-secondary education in any country in the world. Taking a pragmatic approach will foster judgements being made against expectations: that is, addressing any underlying concerns of stakeholders about the *fitness for purpose* of offerings by the sector.[5]

A focus on outcomes is important, but it is unwise to be too narrow when making judgements. The quality of inputs and processes is important too. These inevitably vary, depending on contextual considerations and diversity in programmes, students and staff.

Bearing these points in mind, the particular elements in selection of indicators include:

1 Reliability and transparency.
2 Auditability.
3 Importance and timeliness.
4 The nature of data collected, and their interpretation and use.

Performance indicators provide signals for monitoring developments and performance, examining issues, and assisting in assessment of quality. They can be used to identify good practice, select benchmarking partners, and share best practice information for the benefit of the whole sector. Their relevance varies for different interest groups.

Limitations on use of indicators

There are limitations in current indicators that look at outcomes, and additional indicators should be developed. Understanding the long-term outcomes (the impact of post-secondary education) provides even more challenges in indicator development. For example, impact can be gauged by five-yearly studies of alumni to monitor their satisfaction with their course, or other longitudinal studies such as what use has been made of research findings or scholarly publications. Valid and reliable data and information must be collected. Another problem is posed by information systems which may lead to too much precision, thereby focusing attention on the minutiae of the data, rather than on the information gained by triangulation of data from a range of sets.

To promote judicious use of data, and raise awareness of the importance of context and diversity, it is necessary to develop a framework from which to hang indicators, which will facilitate aggregation of information relating to the post-secondary education sector. A broad sweep approach at the outset will provide guidance for closer examination where required. There can be a *systems and objectives* approach which demands indicators that address missions and goals, or an *activities* approach. There is evidence of a move to preference for performance indicators which are related to objectives, not merely to activities in areas such as teaching and learning, or gender issues. In either case, indicators must be accurate and consistent, and the data must be used to provide information related to the indicators.[6]

Figures 5.3 and 5.4 illustrate other influences on the sector and its objectives. They provide a framework for the use of indicators for inputs, processes and activities and outcomes (outputs and impact).

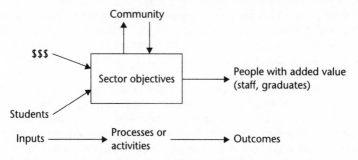

Figure 5.3   Influences on post-secondary education objectives.

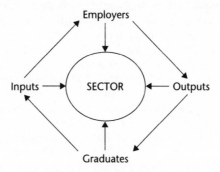

Figure 5.4   Major sources of influence on the post-secondary education sector.

The inputs and expectations (outcomes) themselves combine with feedback from graduates and employers to assist the sector to demonstrate improvement.

Another dimension to indicators encompasses those related to more specific efficiency measures. In Germany there are a number of financial indicators, including:

• productivity ratios;
• output;
• technical efficiency of resources;
• return on input;
• cost of output;
• economy of output and input ratios.

When aggregated with data on equity and diversity, the information from financial indicators may be used to respond to performance indicators which link efficiency to effectiveness.

Staff profile information is important. Monitoring of the characteristics of new staff may be clouded by counting contract staff who
renew contracts, thereby giving a false picture of staff turnover. Both
academic and general staff have an impact on teaching and learning
and research and development, so their qualifications, experience and
the value they bring to their respective positions should be known.
Indicators which can provide evidence for rewarding excellence and
innovation in teaching and learning should be as transparent as those
commonly used to reward research and scholarship (e.g. publications,
grants received, keynote lectures at international conferences).

Indicators for the quality of student services, such as housing,
health service and child care (for staff and students), will become
increasingly important. So will quality indicators for off-shore, international, transnational delivery and twinning programmes, as well
as campuses overseas. Merely having a sector-wide *code of conduct*
is inadequate if there is no audit process. An indicator to force collection of information on the proportion of students who graduate
from institutions in other countries without ever visiting them will
provide a more accurate picture of the global post-secondary education sector when triangulated with records of local students studying
abroad. Internationalization of curricula should involve international
experience or an equivalent cultural and lifestyle sampling for language students. It is also relevant for those taking other courses where
students seek to understand a range of issues which will impact on
them in another country or if they are eventually working in a
multinational company, including cross-cultural communication and
language.[7]

Maintaining quality in an environment of decreasing funding
requires a greater focus at all levels on improving efficiency and
effectiveness. The aim is to make better use of resources to improve
efficiency focusing on the quantitative aspects of process and performance, and to address the qualitative aspects of improving effectiveness, assuring increased levels of client satisfaction. Efficiency
indicators illustrate the extent to which each operational unit –
faculty, department, school (and thereby the education institution)
– meets the measurable components of its objectives (outputs).
Effectiveness indicators relate inputs to outcomes (impact) without
focusing on activities, in order to determine the achievement of the
education institution's objectives in the qualitative sense.

For each operational unit to inform institutional planning, an
annual review of progress towards targets, with commentary on how
they are addressing their own strategic plans, or how they fit into
the institution's plans, should be undertaken. Databases facilitating
collection of information directly from staff via personal computers,

and aggregation of information on performance against indicators and targets for the goals and objectives (e.g. teaching and learning, equity, international and community programmes and research performance indicators), are critical to the success of an annual review. The development and implementation of an executive information system facilitates operational units' ability to extract and manipulate information held in the institution's administrative systems, and more readily to inform planners, on an annual basis, of their performance.

Criteria which should be addressed in each institution's framework or plan for quality management include:

- leadership (driver and enabler);
- policy and planning (enablers), e.g. human resources or workforce plan, financial plan, capital management plan, information plan, equity plan;
- information and analysis (enablers);
- people (enabler, develop and use full potential);
- client focus (driver and enabler);
- quality of process, product and service (key processes);
- organizational performance (outcomes).

Guidelines for the development of quantitative and qualitative performance indicators for each operational unit can be provided, as illustrated by the following example.

Leadership and commitment to quality practices (from the top):
- Managers understand the institution's quality improvement practices and promote them.
- Managers lead by example and seek best practice.
- Programmes for development of staff for continuous improvement are in place, and outcomes monitored.
- Dissemination of information is evident, and best practice is rewarded.

Policies and plans are in place and processes established to evaluate and review them:
- Budget allocation is sufficient and reviewed regularly to enable and ensure the achievement of planned strategic initiatives and targets.
- Programme and planning review processes are structured and on-going, and assist the operational unit to progress to targets, which are reviewed annually allowing revision of plans and targets.
- Relevant plans and policies are established and systematically reviewed.

Information is sought from stakeholders (internal and external clients), the data are analysed and findings are used:
- Institutional surveys determine satisfaction levels of stakeholders.
- Analysis of surveys provides information to all levels of the institution for improvement of processes and practices.
- Annual reviews and surveys are used as tools to determine best practice and provide benchmarks for continuous improvement.

Staff development plans provide for ongoing enhancement of full potential:
- Budget is in place to facilitate orientation for new staff and upgrading of staff qualifications; study leave; short and long training courses.
- Added value is discerned through analyses of outcomes from enhancement activities (e.g. through staff and student satisfaction surveys).
- Continuous quality improvement in staff practices results in stakeholder satisfaction, to the benefit of the institution (i.e. more students of higher standard who are more satisfied and more highly sought by employers).

Stakeholders' needs and desires are sought, anticipated and responded to for service success:
- Feedback is sought regularly and information analysed.
- Results of analyses are disseminated to relevant people and are used for continuous improvement.
- Benchmarks are set and best practices identified to encourage further continuous improvement in provision of services and outcomes.

The institution's processes, products and service in teaching and learning, research and international and community interactions are evaluated and reviewed to ensure continuous improvement of quality:
- The plans relating to the institution's major goals espouse this objective.
- Procedures are in place to monitor improvement and progress towards targets in strategic plans (through annual reviews, five- or six-yearly programme and planning reviews and the use of performance indicators).

Organizational performance is driven by commitment to a systematic approach to continuous improvement of outcomes (through the use of process improvement tools, best practice surveys and benchmarking):
- Benchmarking results in the closing of gaps and movement of baselines.
- Best practices are increasing in number and scope.
- Stakeholder satisfaction is of benefit to the institution (financially and by reputation).
- Staff demonstrate commitment and are more satisfied.

Focusing on outcomes ▪

Quality assurance audits of post-secondary education institutions have raised awareness of a number of issues. Publications in the UK and Australia provide summaries on the strengths and matters for improvement found during audits in those countries.[8] Meade has analysed audit reports and found common themes under five headings:

1 Institutional quality systems.
2 Staff policies and procedures.
3 Papers and programmes.
4 Teaching, learning and assessment.
5 Research and teaching.[9]

For the themes which relate to the key mission of post-secondary education, teaching, learning, assessment and research, matters needing improvement were related to service to clients. These matters are:

- improve the planning of student workloads;
- improve assessment methods;
- strengthen processes which facilitate learning for understanding (transformations);
- improve resources for postgraduate students;
- improve the standard of postgraduate supervision.

This is a challenge for leaders at all levels in post-secondary education institutions, who are urged to adopt *learning organization* strategies and encourage change to ensure continuous improvement. If a quality system is only about assurance and not about improvement in all contexts, it will not serve the education institution well in the global market place. Figure 5.5 represents the key elements of a *quality system*.

High-quality outcomes depend on ever-increasing quality of inputs and throughputs. While the balance is not maintained, the output quality will fall and less than satisfactory outcomes will impact on the graduates, the workforce and thereby the institution. An example can be provided for research indicators where: inputs are researchers, postgraduate students, resources (such as time, money through grants and fellowships, equipment, consumables and so on); throughputs include research projects, research training, candidacy applications and research supervision; and outputs are quantifiable as research

Figure 5.5 Key elements in a quality system.

reports, commercial products, publications, theses, conference papers and presentations. To these, efficiency and effectiveness indicators may be applied (provided they are linked to the institution's vision, mission and research goal, as well as any specific strategies).

Effectiveness indicators include:

1 Level of infrastructure, grants, external funding to support research.
2 Number of staff with research training.
3 Number of new appointments with research training.
4 Demand for postgraduate places.
5 Level of postgraduate student satisfaction, and earnings of post-graduates.
6 Number of new technology transfer ventures.

For these, short- and long-term targets and specific measures should be established. Standard research effectiveness indicators are:

• annual research performance index points by range of programmes;
• annual research income compared with other similar programmes and aggregated to compare with like institutions;

- annual publications by individual, programme and institution compared with others.

Efficiency indicators usually provide information about costs or productivity levels, e.g.

1 Research expenditure per research index point.
2 Research performance points per full-time equivalent (FTE) academic staff member.
3 Research income per *n* (e.g. ten) FTE academic staff compared with other like institutions.
4 Number of publications per *n* FTE academic staff compared with other like institutions.

As previously indicated, impact is more difficult to measure. Where possible, indicators should be developed that go beyond outputs and outcomes to provide information about who uses the publications, the usefulness of research findings, the extent of value to industry, to the professions, to the community and to increasing the knowledge-base in the area. That is, what improvement was made, and does it matter?

It has been established that important elements in improvement are the quality of inputs, throughputs and outputs, as was originally proposed by the father of quality, Deming. However, Deming believed that competition among employees was wrong, preferring cooperation. He despised the notion that individuals could be ranked and rewarded according to performance, which he said defied measurement. Therefore, in relation to staff, he had no time for performance indicators or targets, performance appraisal or merit pay. He argued that evaluating the past performance of individuals could be destructive and unrelated to future improvement, exhorting managers to drive out fear and remove all forms of appraisal. Instead, he suggested they embrace performance enhancement programmes, and reward problem-solving, team contributions and continuous improvement.

On this cautionary note concerning measuring and rewarding the performance of staff, the importance of aspiring to best practice (contextually determined) through the use of benchmarking is the topic of Chapter 6. Understanding where the benchmarks can be found, and moving to enhance performance, is more likely to be rewarding for everyone, and to provide an advantage to the post-secondary education sector as a whole.

6

BENCHMARKING AND BEST PRACTICE

Introduction

Now that the frameworks, principles and guidelines for quality management in post-secondary education have been articulated, more specific information on tools for monitoring performance and improvement are provided in this chapter. Common terms used in relation to quality management include *benchmarking* and *best practice*. This chapter provides information on types of benchmarking and their benefits. It also suggests the rationale and articulates best practice principles and guidelines for integrating them at all levels of operation in post-secondary education institutions. Examples of best practice checklists are provided for guidance when monitoring performance, determining benchmarks and constructing reward mechanisms and policies.

Benchmarking: a tool or a process?

Benchmarking is a quality management tool used when comparing one organization with another on some aspect of performance. Aspects of performance include processes, products and services. Searching to find information on these various aspects in which another organization excels, with the objective of finding ways in which to improve current performance, is benchmarking. A benchmark or standard can be established against which an organization's or institution's own performance can be assessed.

Approaches to the use of benchmarking may be strategic or operational. A strategic approach takes a high-level view and looks at *what is done*, including the organization's business strategy, structure and operational costs. In operational benchmarking, the focus shifts from what is done to *how it is done*. Those processes that are critical to the success of the organization at a number of levels are examined in this approach.[1]

Typology of benchmarking

There are four common types of benchmarking.

1 *Internal benchmarking*: comparing similar processes performed in different parts of the organization to identify better and best practice. For example, internal systems for reviewing curricula, or service-teaching arrangements between one faculty, department or division and another.
2 *Competitive benchmarking*: comparing the performance of one organization (e.g. education institution) with that of a competitor on specific measurable terms. Comparing similar processes, practices, performance measures and identifying trends, directions and priorities, across competitor organizations. For example, measuring student outcomes (e.g. pass rates, satisfaction ratings) compared with how throughput and satisfaction rates are tracked in other public or private education institutions which are recognized for best practice for this process.
3 *Functional benchmarking*: excluding direct competitors, organizations compare processes, practices and performance with similar processes (etc.) of other organizations in the same industry or business, e.g. financial management, library services and student enrolments in education institutions worldwide.
4 *Generic benchmarking*: comparing organizations on a basic practice, process or service, e.g. speed of telephone response, accuracy of payroll, time taken to order and receive an item; or benchmarking student services, such as registry procedures, with private enterprise organizations, e.g. hotels.

To be effective, benchmarking must be used in a structured procedure which follows a number of simple steps:

1 Fully understand the process, product or service to be benchmarked. This may involve a detailed process analysis as a starting point. It will always involve the collection of appropriate output measures.
2 Using the output measures as a comparator, identify organizations which appear to have superior performance and select one or more as benchmarking partners.

3 Study the process, product or service of the benchmarking partner(s) to determine if performance is superior and why.
4 Use this learning to improve.

Benefits of benchmarking

Benefits gained through benchmarking include:

- gaining ideas for improving processes and services from better or best organizations;
- sharing knowledge and experience with others performing the same processes and practices in providing services or products that are critical to success;
- turning the focus towards efficiency and effectiveness to ensure that processes and practices are competitive and to improve planning for targets and the management of resources;
- identifying the *gap* between the organization's performance and that of other organizations to provide the opportunity of closing or increasing the gap;
- continuous improvement as identified by clients and through performance information.

The diagrams in Figure 6.1 provide examples of benchmarking performance in non-academic and academic areas through identifying gaps.

What is best practice?

The principles of best practice based on attention to the learning from benchmarking involve a cooperative effort to recognize the following:

1 Stakeholders, especially students, play a central role in the definition of product (course or programme) and service quality.
2 The institution and its stakeholders work in partnership to achieve improvement in outcomes.
3 Quality derives from well planned and managed processes.
4 An understanding of variation by management is supported by appropriate facts and data.
5 Continuous improvement is part of the management of all processes.
6 Creation and innovation is recognized where it complements continuous improvement.

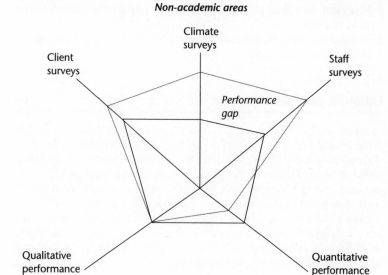

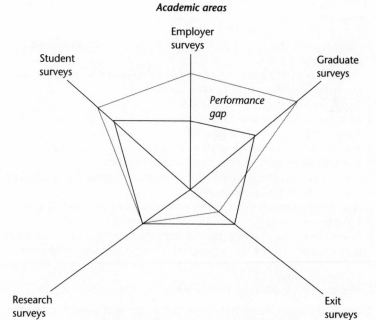

Figure 6.1 Examples of benchmarking performance.

7 Management emphasis is on prevention and improvement rather than reaction.
8 Community and environmental responsibility is considered in the institution's activities.

Rationale and guidelines for achieving best practice

In order to integrate best practice principles, the following guide provides a list of key points to be addressed, and a checklist for each for assessing compliance. Guidelines are best developed at the institutional level. However, faculties, divisions and operational units (schools and departments) should interpret the criteria within their own structure and context to work through the guide.

Under each list of best practice principles relating to seven key points, questions targeted to specific elements are presented in checklists. Each question should be answered contextually, and in the light of the institution's diverse needs.

Best practice key point 1: Leadership

The leader should:

1 Provide clear strategic directions, communicate the vision, inspire and influence staff.
2 Create an environment for quality practices and management, such as ethical decision-making processes.
3 Reinforce the values of the institution.
4 Promote improvement and facilitate change by putting in place approaches, systems and structures, including reward mechanisms.
5 Pursue strategies for involving all levels of management in the integration of quality into day-to-day activities.
6 Encourage involvement with the broader community, including the international community.
7 Assess the extent to which the practices and principles of quality have become integrated within the institution.
8 Assess the extent to which the institution's values have been adopted and become part of the way in which activities are conducted.

Leadership (best practice checklist)

1 *Senior executives* (vice-chancellor, president, CEO, DVCs, executive directors, deans)

(a) What training do senior executives have in quality management principles?
(b) Do senior executives promote quality management principles?
(c) How are institutional values introduced and reinforced through leadership at the executive level?
(d) How are senior executives involved in managing change and implementing a quality culture?
(e) What initiatives do senior executives take to promote unity of purpose and eliminate departmental barriers within the institution?

2 *Management involvement*
(a) What key strategies for involving all levels of management and supervision in quality principles, management, practices and procedures are taken?
(b) What are the principal roles and responsibilities at each level?
(c) How are quality principles integrated into day-to-day management activities, including meetings, decision-making and planning?
(d) What steps are taken by management to assess the effectiveness of its approaches and to improve or change its approaches to integrate quality into day-to-day management?

3 *Community leadership*
(a) How does the institution incorporate ethics, social justice, equity, occupational health and safety and environmental responsibility into its policies and practices?
(b) To what extent are staff engaged in the promotion of quality awareness in the sharing of experience and knowledge and in other quality-related activities among community, business, trade, education, health and government or other external organizations?
(c) How does the institution and its senior management encourage such staff involvement?

Best practice key point 2: Strategy, policy and planning

Senior executives and managers should:

1 Generate values that reflect best practice principles.
2 Translate values and implement them in daily operations.

3 Involve the institution's community, both internal and external, in the development of the institution's values.

Policy and planning (best practice checklist)

1 *Integration of organizational values*
   (a) How do employees at all levels contribute to the development of the institution's values and related policies?
   (b) Are the institution's values clearly reflected in its vision and mission, objectives, policies and guidelines, and are they incorporated in best practice principles?
   (c) Are the institution's values communicated effectively to all employees at every level?
   (d) Are all employees at every level involved in ongoing communication and deployment of values and policies?
   (e) Can the institution's values be seen to have affected all its operations?
   (f) Does the institution measure the acceptance of and commitment to its values?

2 *The planning process* (how strategic plans are developed and deployed via business planning, operational planning and action plans to achieve the best use of resources)
   (a) How does the institution incorporate its values in plans and associated indicators to track performance?
   (b) How does the institution use the planning process to operationalize its values?
   (c) How are the needs of all stakeholders used in the development of plans and key indicators?
   (d) What is the role of employees at all levels in the development of plans?
   (e) Are short-term and long-term goals prioritized at all levels in relation to the institution's plan?
   (f) Do high-level short-term and long-term plans contain implementation strategies, performance measures, critical success factors and targets, and resource allocation commitments (e.g. people, physical, technological, financial, information)?
   (g) Are goals and principles relating to quality incorporated into the planning process?
   (h) Is the focus for improvement aligned to strategic objectives?
   (i) Are client and stakeholder requirements, student and staff capabilities, competitive and benchmark data used in the development of plans, policies and objectives?

(j) Is the effectiveness of planning processes and implementation of plans monitored, evaluated and reviewed?

Best practice key point 3: Information and analysis

There should be evidence of:

1 Appropriate data and information which are valid and of high quality.
2 Competitive comparisons and benchmarks.
3 Analysis and use of data and information.
4 Organizational performance indicators.

Information and analysis (best practice checklist)

1 *Scope and collection of data and information*
  (a) What criteria are used for data and information selection, and how are the types of data linked to plans?
  (b) How are data reliability, consistency, standardization, timeliness, and access reviewed?
  (c) What steps are taken to evaluate and improve the reliability, consistency, standardization, cycle time, analysis and dissemination of data?

2 *Benchmarking*
  (a) Are comparative performance data collected?
  (b) Is there any involvement in benchmarking processes?
  (c) Are best practices found and adopted?
  (d) Are the processes for collecting such data, involvement in benchmarking and adopting best practice evaluated?

3 *Analysis and use of data and information*
  (a) Have steps been taken to develop the understanding of statistical and other tools for the analysis of data, including trend data?
  (b) Are variations reflected in key policies and activities?
  (c) How are assessment, and improvement of analysis and use of data, evaluated?

4 *Organizational performance indicators*
  (a) Are measures and indicators established to monitor performance; how are these reported and used in review and planning processes?
  (b) Are these measures used to predict future performance targets?
  (c) Are trends analysed and conclusions drawn to inform the planning process?

Best practice key point 4: People

Management should:

1 Create an environment conducive to participation, trust, teamwork, empowerment, personal leadership, personal growth and pride in performance.
2 Create an environment that enables the full potential of staff to be realized.
3 Involve staff at all levels (including casual) in day-to-day activities and continuous improvement.
4 Align human resource management objectives with the institution's objectives and strategic directions.

People (best practice checklist)

1 *Human resource management planning*
   (a) Are human resource plans integrated with the institution's plan, the vision, mission, goals and value statements, objectives, policies and guidelines?
   (b) Are human resource priorities related to the institution's priorities, including key strategies to increase the involvement, effectiveness, productivity and satisfaction of the organization's people?
   (c) What processes are in place to evaluate and improve human resource planning?

2 *Staff involvement*
   (a) Does the institution provide for and respond to teamwork, suggestion schemes and other forms of staff participation initiatives?
   (b) What specific mechanisms empower staff to act, take initiatives and accept responsibility?
   (c) Has the concept of the *internal client* been promoted and used?
   (d) What principal indicators are used to evaluate the extent and effectiveness of staff involvement, and how are these indicators (including trend data) used?

3 *Performance management*
   (a) Is a performance management system in place that recognizes and rewards individuals and groups?
   (b) Do the institution's staff development processes include career-path planning?

(c) Are the above processes and systems related to the institution's value statements and objectives?

(d) Is the effectiveness of performance management systems and processes evaluated, with findings used to improve strategies and plans in these areas?

4 *Education and training*
   (a) Do the approach and rationale used to decide the education and training needed by staff link directly to the institution's strategic directions and plans, including:
   - skills training;
   - multi-skilling;
   - use of process control and improvement;
   - general education for future needs?

   (b) Are statistics and costing maintained on staff education and training?

   (c) Are processes in place to improve, and to assess the effectiveness of, the institution's education and training activities?

5 *Well-being and morale*
   (a) Does the institution measure key indicators and trends in staff well-being and morale?

   (b) What action is taken to resolve identified problems and weaknesses, in matters such as:
   - absenteeism;
   - staff turnover;
   - satisfaction;
   - grievances;
   - strikes;
   - workers' compensation claims?

   (c) Do staff mobility, flexibility and retraining support the transition to new technologies, and lead to improved productivity or changes in work processes?

   (d) What special facilities, services and opportunities exist at the institution for staff, e.g.
   - counselling;
   - assistance (e.g. child care, health services, financial services);
   - recreational or cultural facilities;
   - non-work-related educational opportunities?

   (e) How are issues like safety and health, staff satisfaction and ergonomics included in improvement activities; what goals, methods and trends are identified?

   (f) How are internal or external environmental changes managed to promote the well-being of the institution's staff?

6 *Communication*
   (a) What principal mechanisms exist for communication between management and staff?
   (b) What types of information are provided and how frequently?
   (c) What processes are established for communication among staff?
   (d) Have special initiatives taken place to address the quality focus (such as discussion and information forums)?
   (e) Are communication processes evaluated for effectiveness; are supporting data gathered to reflect trends?

Best practice key point 5: Client focus

Management should:

1 Anticipate, identify, respond to and satisfy the needs and expectations of the institution's external clients.
2 Reinforce the importance of external clients throughout the institution's operations.
3 Develop and improve the institution's external client interface processes.
4 Improve and seek further to improve client satisfaction and loyalty.

Client focus (best practice checklist)

1 *Knowledge of clients' needs and expectations*
   (a) Are mechanisms in place to determine clients' current and future requirements; to identify their relative importance?
   (b) Are market and environmental-scanning data used?
   (c) How are identified requirements communicated to relevant areas throughout the institution?
   (d) What methods are used to ensure that requirements are understood, to assess effectiveness of the processes used and to collect data to show improvements?

2 *Client relationship management*
   (a) How does the institution evaluate the following:
      • client relations' management;
      • accuracy in responding to queries;
      • timeliness of feedback and responses;
      • client satisfaction?
   (b) How are these factors used to improve training, technology, customer-focused management practices?

3 *Client satisfaction*
   (a) Has the quality of product (e.g. courses, research findings, publications) and service (e.g. consultancy) been linked to trend shifts in market share?
   (b) How is such information used in the institution, and what are the resulting actions and consequences?
   (c) Is client satisfaction compared or benchmarked with others, internally, or against national and international competitors?

Best practice key point 6: Quality of process, product and service

Management should:

1 Understand the processes, products and services provided.
2 Empower staff to be innovative and creative in undertaking processes and delivering products and services to the satisfaction of clients.
3 Continuously evaluate the effectiveness of its processes, products and services to improve performance.
4 Embrace quality management in all operations which affect the delivery of products and services.

Quality of process, product and service (best practice checklist)

1 *Design and innovation*
   (a) How does the institution create, discover and evaluate new techniques and technologies?
   (b) How do such activities assist the achievement of sufficiently high levels of performance?
   (c) How does the institution encourage and enable innovation throughout its operations, in the design of its courses, in services and in the improvement of its core processes in teaching and learning and research?
   (d) Are the needs of students and other stakeholders incorporated into the design or redesign of courses and services?
   (e) What methods ensure that quality is built in at all stages of the creation of new courses and services?
   (f) How does the institution evaluate and improve the effectiveness of its designs and design processes so that the introduction of new courses and services progressively improves the quality of these *products* to meet established sufficiently high performance standards and the needs of clients?

2 *Supplier (secondary education sector and recruiting) relations and quality improvement*
   (a) What is the supplier relationship process – how are suppliers chosen and relationships established?
   (b) Does the institution involve suppliers and other education sectors in improvement processes?

3 *Management and improvement of processes*
   (a) What standards does the institution recognize and uphold?
   (b) To what extent has the institution been successful in meeting such requirements or what progress has been achieved?
   (c) How has compliance to meet performance criteria been incorporated into the institution's overall quality improvement effort?
   (d) What principal approaches does the institution use to assess quality of product and service?
   (e) With reference to key performance quality indicators, what evidence is there of improvement?
   (f) What key measures exist for evaluating process performance and improvement in:
      • human resource management?
      • capital management?
      • budget management?
      • research indices?
      • teaching indices?
      • student progress data?
   (g) Are these key measures used in determining the effectiveness of improvements, to provide evidence of, and to enhance, improvement?
   (h) Does the institution incorporate the standardization of procedures into operations and how are these standards continually reviewed?
   (i) How is the effectiveness of quality systems and quality practices reviewed, audited and improved?
   (j) How does product and service performance compare with competitors and world-class performance?

Best practice key point 7: Organizational performance

Management should ensure that:

1 Value is added to the organization and its stakeholders.
2 Benefits are gained for all stakeholders.
3 Financial performance is improved.

Organizational performance (best practice checklist)

1 *Results and outcomes*
   (a) How does the institution evaluate the depth and breadth of initiatives towards achieving best practice and the extent to which aims were achieved?
   (b) For each defined indicator, were trend data gathered?
   (c) Where appropriate, are results compared or benchmarked with similar national and international organizations?
   (d) How are data on performance indicators used to monitor *business risks* that could impact on the institution's performance?

2 *Improvement*
   (a) How does the institution review the effectiveness and appropriateness of the approaches described and their deployment, and build on the knowledge gained to improve continually?

Example of a best practice checklist (research)

An area in post-secondary education not dealt with under *processes* in Chapter 4 is research. Although more usually undertaken in universities, research is becoming more evident in the vocational education sector. In the checklist provided for research performance, the questions should be answered and the responses should be open to scrutiny and audit. Some of the headings under which best practice can be assessed in research are presented not merely as indicators of performance, but to identify areas of excellence. They include:

Applications for grants
• How many applications per year?
• What percentage of full-time equivalent (FTE) staff applied?
• How many were successful?

Grants received
• How many?
• What percentage of FTE staff were successful?
• What was the range and average value?

Nature of grants
• International, competitive?
• National, competitive?
• Peer-reviewed?
• Industry?
• Institutional?

Other research income
- Fellowships?
- Post-doctoral awards or scholarships?
- Non-peer-reviewed grants and awards?
- Professional practice?
- Editorships and editorial boards (scholarly journals)?
- Marketed research products?
- Internal PhDs completed under supervision and associate supervision?
- Internal professional doctorates completed under supervision and associate supervision?
- Masters as above?
- PhD and research masters examined?
- Chairing or organizing major national or international conferences?
- National and international research presentations (abstracts and posters)?
- Presentations at local, state and district conferences?
- Research reports to client groups (discussion papers)?
- Artistic productions or performances?
- Prestigious awards, publications, medals for research performance?
- Keynote or plenary lectures and awards for best papers and presentations (at national and international conferences)?
- Membership of national and international decision-making panels for research grants and awards applications?
- Membership of other decision-making panels for research grants and awards applications?
- Reviews of external research grant applications?
- Refereeing journal articles and conference proceedings?

Research output
- Books authored (research)?
- Books authored (other)?
- Books edited?
- Books revised or new editions?
- Book chapters?
- Journal articles (scholarly refereed)?
- Journals: other contributions (scholarly refereed)?
- Journals: non-refereed articles (including professional journals)?
- Journals: letters or notes?
- Major reviews?
- Conference publications: full written papers, refereed proceedings?
- Conference publications: full written papers, non-refereed proceedings?
- Conference publications: extracts of papers?

- Conference publications: edited volumes of conference proceedings?
- Audio-visual recordings and CDs?
- Computer software?
- Technical drawings or architectural designs and working models?
- Patents?
- Other creative works: major written or recorded works?
- Other creative works: minor written or recorded works?
- Other creative works: individual exhibitions of original art?
- Other creative works: representations of original art?
- Exhibitions curated?

Annual performance can be assessed and best practice examples identified. Expected performance will vary contextually. Any benchmarks that are set should be for similar areas and potential for performance weighted. For example, large competitive grants and other funds from drug companies are more readily available to medical, dentistry and veterinary researchers. Few large grants are available for researchers in the humanities. Development of a set of performance indices in each education institution is a starting point for highlighting where best practice examples can be found. The index will also provide a means to reward performance if points are allocated in each category and money is assigned to each point according to the available recurrent funding each year. Provided a weighting mechanism is in place to ensure some level of equity, and auditing of claims is undertaken to assure the authenticity and quality of submissions, research and scholarly effort will be seen to be valued.

Postgraduate training best practice checklist

At a nexus point between research and teaching is the area of postgraduate research training. Best practice in this context involves considering a number of factors which will ensure that students' postgraduate experience is rewarding, and inspires them to apply for post-doctoral awards or continue the research effort in their chosen area. As wages and salaries rise, more opportunities for consultancies become available and bright young PhD-holders are poached by industry and commerce, research institutes and universities are experiencing a *brain drain*. This is particularly the case in nations where low salaries and less than excellent research conditions pertain.

Building an environment which is stimulating and rewarding, through attending to the standard of facilities and the range of interactions, and by providing opportunities, will facilitate satisfaction for the clients. As Neville and French point out, students and supervisors should negotiate their expectations early in their relationship.[2] By communicating needs, possible difficulties can be identified. In a useful publication by McDonald and colleagues, the importance of understanding at all stages of involvement with postgraduate students is shown to be important for their personal and professional growth.[3]

The following checklist of questions can be used to consider elements likely to be of relevance to postgraduate training. It can also provide guidelines for establishing a policy which will foster best practice.

Requirements for appointment of postgraduate supervisor
• Higher level of training?
• Active involvement in the area of the student's research?
• Experience and education in supervisory skills?
• Identified competence?
• Time allowance?

Research environment
• Conducive to research?
• Challenging?
• Intellectually stimulating?
• Supportive and nurturing?
• Safe, healthy, without harassment, discrimination or conflict?

Procedures and regulations
• Policies and procedures are in place related to research and research training?
• Do supervisors and students know of them?
• Support available in relation to policies, e.g. on harassment, race relations, special needs (disabilities, language and cultural requirement)?

Relationships
• Choice of a supervisor mutual and informed?
• Academic integrity, maturity, professionalism and objectivity?
• Dependence, sexual, gender and other issues, such as animosity, avoided?
• Official guidelines on research ethics and conflicts of interest followed?

Programme development
• Guidance provided to students on selection, design, planning and conduct of a topic?
• Assistance with equipment, laboratory instruments, techniques, experimental models and animals?
• Research methodology and statistical analysis courses available?
• Assistance with interpretation of raw data provided?

- Direction on writing, defending, submitting and publishing given?
- Knowledge of the department, opportunities to liaise with others, relevant seminars conveyed?

Consultation and advice
- Regular meetings?
- Timelines on submission and return of work and other expectations agreed?
- Feedback given on work undertaken, including written work?

Committees and panels
- Faculty, school and department committees in place?
- Expectations known to supervisors and students, e.g. regarding candidacy requirements, progress reports?

Facilities
- Space, desk, chair, storage, secure files, computer, software available?
- Email and Internet connections in place?
- Sources and levels of available funding known, e.g. for conference attendance?
- Resources available, e.g. photocopying, printing, library searches, library holdings?

Intellectual property and publications
- Encouragement to present at seminars and conferences and to publish?
- Clarification on rights of supervisor and student on acknowledgement when presenting or publishing?
- Policy on intellectual property in place, known and observed?

Other matters
- Provisions made for leave of absence requests?
- Alternative supervisors available when staff take leave?
- Grievance procedures?
- Conflict resolution process?
- Student charter?
- Paid work available?

While this checklist is not exhaustive, it does provide guidelines for consideration of best practice and evaluation of performance in the area of postgraduate research training.[4]

Best practice in teaching

It is more difficult to measure performance and identify best practice by establishing indices for teaching. Many universities have adopted a model of using a teaching portfolio or dossier to identify areas of best practice and provide rewards. Highlighting the importance of understanding clients' needs through seeking results of student surveys of satisfaction with teaching, courses, learning opportunities and materials, responsiveness, feedback, supervision skills, mentoring and assessment is common to all portfolios. Others require evidence of innovative approaches to teaching and learning (such as interactive multimedia packages), reflective practice, good teaching awards, research into teaching and learning, internationalization of curricula, equity provisions, responsiveness to diversity issues and presentations at conferences on teaching and learning.[5]

Another element of best practice in post-secondary education is whether teachers have formal qualifications in education. Many have a PhD in their professional area, and are highly valued for their knowledge and experience in the domains in which they teach, but do not know how to teach. There is a move to insist that those who are employed to teach on higher education programmes possess some sort of formal teaching qualification.[6] Necessarily, recognition of prior learning and experience, coupled with documented evidence of exemplary performance as measured by feedback from clients, will be allowed for those seeking exemption from any requirements.

Feedback on client satisfaction and best practice

All post-secondary education institutions must seek client feedback. This is generally obtained through surveys of students and graduates, and by asking employers whether the attributes of graduates are relevant in the workplace. While this feedback is readily sought from industry, health providers, businesses and commercial enterprises, those graduates who are self-employed or pursuing further study and research should also be queried. Assuming that there are objectives in teaching and learning plans that relate to the attributes valued by an institution, and therefore to be addressed in courses, deciding on a list of attributes is important. All those likely to benefit – employers, currently employed graduates, graduates pursuing other interests, studying or in self-employment – should be involved in discussions. There may be generic attributes, but there will certainly be specific attributes for each profession or function, e.g. medicine, teacher education, engineering, mine surveying, computer science, information technology, pharmacy, law, marketing, architecture, art and drama, to name a few.[7]

Assessing the attributes of graduates to confirm best practice ▮

There are few studies on surveys of employer satisfaction. One which sought employers' perception of whether graduates in their employment demonstrated lifelong learning skills and work-related skills, and the extent to which graduate skills related to specific degree objectives, was conducted by Meade and Andrews.[8] This particular survey was an extension of the work of Ramsden and associates on the Graduate Careers Council of Australia's Course Experience Questionnaire (CEQ).[9] It was also based on the concepts of lifelong learning espoused by Candy and associates in a commissioned report to the National Board of Employment, Education and Training in Australia.[10]

In developing Meade and Andrews's employer survey, attention was paid to findings from a seminar at the University of Warwick in the United Kingdom. In this seminar, speakers, addressing the topic 'employer views in higher education', highlighted difficulties they had in conducting employer surveys, including response rates of less than 10 per cent.[11]

Meade, from New Zealand, cites how his team achieved response rates in excess of 70 per cent by locating employers who were well aware of graduates from the university in question, and seeking guidance on specific matters where improvements could be made. The work-related skills that were identified in the first part of the survey included:

- graduates' assertiveness, ambition and desire for self-improvement;
- willingness to accept direction, motivation and positive attitude to work;
- reliability, interpersonal and leadership skills;
- degree of organizational, technical and time management skills;
- understanding of research methodology;
- negotiation skills;
- computer technology skills.[12]

There was no indication of how these attributes were selected, such as whether they were linked to a teaching and learning plan. A second section of the survey, however, did derive items based on the objectives of each programme or whether they were included by the specific department or school.

A third component of the survey asked employers about lifelong learning skills as included in a graduate survey (for cross-referencing) and added three other questions related to self-esteem, a desire to continue learning into the future and skills to find and assess information.

In Australia, results of a pilot study of a graduate attributes survey revealed that graduates were perceived by their employers to be performing less than adequately on some attributes. Such attributes, which included writing skills and time management, can be hypothesized to have been very important to their performance in particular organizations. Further investigation found that these attributes were important to engender in all graduates. Writing skills need to be broken down into categories in order to gain a valid response from employers. It could be suggested that graduates are unaccustomed to writing in the variety of formats that may be required by the office environment. However, those asked to write a discussion paper may be judged to have good writing skills as an attribute because this is a more familiar writing style given their education requirements of assignment preparation. The lack of time management skills could be due to the manner in which university study is more of a self-paced activity, rather than one in which there are daily deadlines towards which to work.

Another attribute that was identified by the survey as being less than adequately developed was *awareness of national and international issues*. Such awareness, which might be of limited relevance to some workplaces, is becoming increasingly important in the global market. Interestingly, this attribute was commonly rated by employers as being non-applicable.

Employers were also able to identify a variety of additional attributes upon which they thought graduates needed to improve. These may be categorized as general and specific attributes that employers identified as being essential to work performance. One general attribute may be considered a skill applicable to graduates independent of their different background: that is, *managerial skills*.

The specific attributes that were identified were those that were applicable to specialized fields of expertise. Such skills and attributes might have limited validity for use in a general survey of graduates, but have great relevance to specific courses and school disciplines. An example of one specific skill identified was the ability to use specialist computer software that is only relevant to that discipline. Individual schools and areas would find the incorporation of these skills into a school-specific section of a graduate attributes survey extremely valuable.

Other attributes identified by employers, such as personal disposition and office skills, might be outside of the influence of post-secondary education programmes. Comments on personal dispositions included graduates' professionalism and attitude to co-workers. Office skills mentioned as needing improvement included being able to use office equipment and schedule meetings, attributes that are not necessarily provided in most courses.

Employers usually commented that a degree provides the start for a career, but does not ensure successful work performance in itself. They are aware of differences between the theoretical and practical knowledge of the graduates, often placing the most value on practical application of knowledge rather than the theoretical background gained through the graduate's course.[13] *The Graduate Employment and Training towards the Millennium (GET) Report* in the UK confirms that employers are interested in so-called soft skills such as problem-solving, verbal and written communication, teamwork and self-management, as well as technical ability.[14]

One of the most positive findings from the Australian study was that employers generally perceived that graduates from the surveying university compared favourably with graduates from other universities. Another useful piece of information for marketing is to discover whether graduates are hired through the traditional means of responding to printed advertisements or submitting applications of interest to employers. Of interest to course coordinators is the number of graduates who are employed as a result of completing work experience or practical assignments in work environments, which would suggest that employers were suitably impressed by the ability of the students to perform in work situations to offer them employment. The manner in which graduates find employment through such avenues adds value to the use of practical work experience as part of the undergraduate course content.

Introducing the topic of marketing leads naturally to the important issue of competition. While most academics strenuously resist the notion that education institutions are businesses, most would agree there is fierce competition for high-quality students and certainly for research grants and other income.

Competitiveness

As government funding decreases and fees increase, the trend to privatization of the sector, and credit or voucher schemes where funding is provided directly to individuals rather than institutions, will see education provision become more competitive. In the USA, public enrolments have increased but the private rates of return on investment are improving when compared with social (public) rates.[15] Both the Dearing Report in the UK and the West Review in Australia have focused on funding models and sources of income from other than government coffers.[16] This is particularly relevant in a climate where there is a proliferation of open and flexible learning packages, and the use of multimedia and other technologies, which will see clients less likely to use a local provider.[17]

It is incumbent on all post-secondary institutions to incorporate some form of quality management system. Integrating criteria, such as those in the ISO 9000 standards, into a total quality management system and using client focus criteria, such as those for the Australian Quality Awards (AQA), the European Quality Awards or the Baldrige Awards in the USA, will ensure that:

- clients' needs and opinions are taken into account;
- a competitive strategy, including knowledge of the competition, is developed;
- the needs of the market are addressed;
- procedures (as simple as possible) to ensure quality performance are in place;
- performance measures are developed;
- processes are reviewed continuously to eliminate waste;
- effective communication is ensured;
- evidence of continuous improvement is sought.

The last two elements are vital to any quality system. Another factor not often considered in the post-secondary education sector is the cost-effectiveness of the quality system. While a focus on clients is increasing, performance measures which are sensitive to the market will be part of a competitive strategy.[18] There is no doubt that accountability will continue to be expected, and preparedness is a wise course. Knowledge of the interactions between external policies and internal policies and practices will facilitate reporting on best practices and quality improvement through established performance criteria across all post-secondary education institutions.

There is a range of models of quality management, from those involving strict adherence to standards for all phases of an operation and all operations in an organization, to a total focus on quality service to clients (both internal and external). A combination of models is best adaptable to the post-secondary education sector. Chapter 7 provides an overview of a number of models, but there are many more which can be found in the literature and in practice around the globe. There is no intention to recommend the use of particular models, merely to highlight the range of approaches and provide some insight into how various elements of a standards approach and use of best practice criteria may be combined favourably for managing quality in all aspects of post-secondary education.

7

MODELS TO CONSIDER

Introduction

Whilst there may be no particular model of management for quality and standards that is completely applicable to the post-secondary education sector, this chapter provides information on a range which dominates the quality management debate. Adopting the most useful elements of each and adapting them for individual institutions' processes, procedures and practices is suggested. Readers will be interested in the convergence of each model towards focusing on clients and seeking transformation to facilitate improvement.

Total quality management

Total quality management (TQM) is based on assuring the quality of products and services to the satisfaction (and delight) of consumers (customers, clients, students). Frederick Taylor first proposed theories of scientific management which focused beyond the inspection of products at the end of production to testing work methods and seeing end testing as the guarantor of quality.[1]

Radford's work in 1922 established the need for quality assurance inspectors to test every product before it left the factory.[2] For higher education this would equate to requiring an exit exam for students before graduation to test what they had learnt from the course (the product) and how the services (teaching and learning opportunities, research experiences, student services) were delivered. Such a method lends itself to secondary education, but beyond is likely to be an impediment to diversity in the preparation of graduates for a range of professional and industrial occupations, for ongoing research or for artistic scholarly pursuits. Surveys of graduates to ascertain their satisfaction and whether they have gained employment are widespread. Perhaps these provide some evidence of the quality of the product! Triangulation of graduate survey information with the results of surveys of (a) students who exit before completion of courses, (b) results of professional entry examinations, (c) employers to seek information about the suitability of skills and attributes of graduates, (d) alumni over time to assess their acquisition of lifelong learning abilities, and the suitability of their original course for their ongoing careers and continuing education, may have more value.[3]

Taylor's scientific management approach and Radford's quality control inspection were progressed by Shewhart in the late 1920s. In collaboration with W. Edwards Deming, Harold Dodge, G. D. Edwards, Joseph Juran and Harry Romig, he converted statistical methods to a manufacturing discipline for economic control of quality in manufactured products. Deming perfected the method and identified *seven deadly diseases*:

1 Lack of constancy of purpose.
2 Emphasis on short-term profits.
3 Evaluation by performance, merit rating or annual review of performance.
4 Mobility of management.
5 Running a company on visible figures alone.
6 Excessive medical costs for employee health care, which increase the final costs of goods and services.
7 Excessive costs of warranty, fuelled by lawyers who work on the basis of contingency fees.[4]

Deming also espoused his *fourteen points* as TQM principles:

1 Create constancy of purpose for improvement of product or service.
2 Adopt a new philosophy whereby those in management or administrative positions must learn what their responsibilities are and embrace leadership for change.
3 Cease dependence on mass inspection to achieve quality by building quality into the product.
4 End the practice of awarding business on price alone.
5 Constantly improve the production and service system to improve productivity and quality and to decrease costs.
6 Institute training.
7 Institute leadership.

8 Drive out fear.

9 Break down barriers between organizational components.

10 Eliminate slogans, exhortations and numerical targets for the workforce because they are divisive.

11 Eliminate work standards or quotas, management by objectives and other numerical goals.

12 Remove barriers to pride of workmanship.

13 Institute a vigorous programme of education and self-improvement.

14 Put everyone in the company to work to accomplish the trans-formation.[5]

The PDC(S)A (plan, do, check(study), act) cycle for quality management was also devised by Deming. He proposed that moving ahead to improve continuously relies on planning well before doing anything; monitoring and assessment of the success of outcomes; and making necessary changes or adjustments before advancing. The four stages in the cycle behave as chocks to prevent backwards motion.

Juran proposed a trilogy of processes – quality planning, quality control and quality improvement – and emphasized ten stages for total quality:

1 Create awareness of the need and opportunity for quality improvement.

2 Set goals for continuous improvement.

3 Build an organization to achieve goals by establishing a quality council, identifying problems, selecting a project, appointing teams and choosing facilitators.

4 Give everyone training.

5 Carry out projects to solve problems.

6 Report progress.

7 Show recognition.

8 Communicate results.

9 Keep a record of successes.

10 Incorporate annual improvements into the company's regular systems and processes and thereby maintain momentum.[6]

TQM does not involve adherence to strict standards; nor does it focus totally on service quality as the major basis for success of a quality management system. Both of these approaches are presented, with examples and suggested possibilities to articulate some elements of a range of approaches which may be useful in the post-secondary education sector.

Service success models

Research on service quality and success grew strongly in the late 1970s and can be traced to the *Nordic School of Services*, which became a source of information about a range of contributions in service quality models, mainly from Scandinavia.[7] Early research into the management of service operations is also found in the USA in a paper by Sasser, Olsen and Wyckoff.[8] A leading example of success through attention to the quality of service is provided by SAS, the international airline of Sweden, Denmark and Norway.[9]

In 1981, after SAS had posted a loss of US$8 million, its multinational board of directors appointed Jan Carlzon as president. By 1983, SAS was operating with a gross profit of US$70 million and was voted airline of the year. Carlzon approached his task from a marketing point of view. The idea was as simple as it was compelling – to sell what the customer wants to buy. But it involved an essential shift in focus from the production process to the market, and to being customer- and client-driven. His *moments of truth* dictum saw a concerted effort in Scandinavia to discover the ingredients of service management. A moment of truth is any point of contact, direct or indirect, between a customer or client and the company.[10] These moments present the opportunities to manage the customer's or client's experience. But because so many of the moments occurred beyond the purview of managers, they had to learn how to manage them indirectly.[11]

The story of the SAS transformation remained somewhat of a Scandinavian secret until the mid-1980s. Then, in quick succession, Normann in Europe, and Albrecht and Zemke in North America began to elaborate on the service management concept.[12] Concurrently, in Sweden, Gronroos and, in the USA, Parasuraman, Zeithaml and Berry began publishing results of research into the determinants of service quality that had a strong marketing perspective, and proposed models that continued to be developed and fine-tuned in the 1990s.[13] Likewise, Albrecht continued to refine and recast the service management concept into a *total quality service* (TQS) model.[14]

The total quality service model

The TQS model is a framework that brings together a range of practices and shows how they integrate to deliver superior customer and client value through service, and ultimately success for the organization. How each practice is operationalized, how much certain

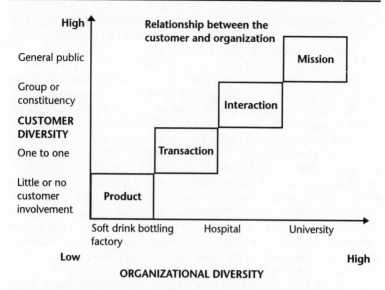

Figure 7.1 Quality service paradigm contingency model.
Source: Adapted from Albrecht (1988, 1990, 1992, 1994).

elements are emphasized or suppressed, depends on the premise an organization is pursuing in relation to how it best creates value for its clients, and by the diversity of its offerings. Figure 7.1 presents one way of viewing such contingency by looking at a spectrum of organizational diversity, and the nature and degree of customer participation in an organization's processes.

At the low end of this organizational and customer diversity spectrum is the situation where a customer buys a product, like a soft drink, and does not interact with its producer. The soft drink bottling factory needs to have management practices that minimize variation and waste, use economies of scale and increase reliability and repetition. The intelligence of this sort of operation is in the design of an effective system which does not require an innovative workforce for it to run. For the customer, value is in the product. There are choices that can be made:

1 To continue using the product.
2 To change brands.
3 To go without.

Increasingly, this type of manufacturing operation is automated and customers service themselves without any need to interact personally with the producing organization.

An example of an organization in the middle of the spectrum is a hospital. In a hospital, some activities have to be undertaken in exactly the same way each time, e.g. inserting an intravenous drip. For this procedure similar sorts of routines and protocols are involved as are required in the bottling plant at the low end of the spectrum. A limited amount of customer and client interaction (apart from a degree of cooperation) is involved. However, other activities and procedures have to be left to the discretion of health experts, such as surgical or therapy teams, who need the latitude to be able to think and problem solve on a case-by-case basis, and respond to different situations. Overall, the value of service in these situations depends on the clients' perception of the manner in which treatment was given and how interactions with them were managed. Patients also make judgements of the quality of technical competence, interpersonal interactions and the physical and procedural features of the hospital. The creation of value is a fusion of concrete and abstract judgements and it is a joint phenomenon involving general employees, nurses, doctors, therapists, paramedics, patients, the patients' families and others.

Albrecht suggests that universities and public service organizations are at the high end of the spectrum, where the customer and client interface is diverse and complex. Management should be mission-driven and focused on successful outcomes, rather than relying on processes and procedures management. Thus post-secondary education institutions should have meaningful concepts of service based on strategies for value creation. They should have in place disciplined means to assess performance, and ways of energizing academic and general staff and clients (students) to believe in them. Indeed, the students, by providing feedback and stimulation for change and continuous improvement, may be considered to be involved as co-producers.[15]

The role of the leader in service success

Even politicians should have some arguable value creation premise for a public sector organization to survive, and they should be involved in developing it. They should take a leading role in developing a vision of the type of public value an organization should create. Executive leadership then becomes a craft of meaning with the aim of maximizing the value creation by conveying and being a living embodiment of a strong message, something that people can relate to and rally around, guiding the organization's efforts to that end.

The message is the same for the post-secondary education and public service sectors. If managers want their front-line staff to treat the clients well, they should treat their front-line staff in the same way. Executives should be willing to support and align the organization's resources behind the front-line staff and always be a living embodiment of the service culture they espouse. Middle managers have to shed their control and compliance garb and instead clothe themselves as facilitators and coaches.

In 1988, Albrecht used the metaphor of turning the traditional pyramid of authority upside down to show that service management was the antithesis of manufacturing management.[16] He went on to explain later how this could be accomplished, particularly by overcoming the resistance of middle managers.[17] The idea of inverting the pyramid originated with Olle Stiwenius, director of Scandinavian Airlines management consultants.[18] It was also featured in later works by Barton and Marson, and Denhardt, relative to the delivery of government services.[19]

Defining service

At its simplest, service is defined as work done by one person for the benefit of another. Like all things though, it derives far greater meaning when put into context. Service exists within a milieu of human values, and the client retains only the memory of an experience. It is the spirit in which the service was given that is remembered. Albrecht defined this spirit of service as an attitude which is based on particular values and beliefs about people, life and work, that inspires people to serve others willingly and take pride in their work.[20] Service as such should not be confused with servitude, where people are compelled *slavishly* to serve others, or where management forces undue adherence to rules or regulations.

Albrecht and Zemke studied examples of outstanding service organizations and came up with five steps to transform a *factory-style* management mentality to a *customer-driven* one.[21] The magnitude of the task is encapsulated in the name of Albrecht's well known chapter 'How to teach an elephant to dance', which prescribes the steps. Albrecht went on to refine the five steps into five phases, in light of business experiences with service management. He refers to service management as a complete organizational approach to ensuring the quality of service, as defined by the customer, as the pre-eminent driving force for operating a business.[22]

Five phases in service success

The five phases are presented as guidelines for those aspiring to successful service.

1 Find out what clients want

This applies equally to paying (external) clients and fellow staff members (internal clients). The strategy involves developing continuous pictures of what success looks like: that is, what satisfies the external client, and what quality of work life (climate) motivates staff to give exemplary levels of service to both external and internal clients. The measurement of market and workplace feelings or perceptions will, of necessity, be more qualitative than that required for product quality. Interviews, focus groups and questionnaires are used to develop the pictures. However, knowledge of special and common causes of variation is still required to interpret the results of such research and to guard against the organization unreasonably chasing whims or even fantasies. It is also useful to establish a service quality task force to maintain advocacy for the effort. The first phase provides the foundation for the second.

2 Clarify a service strategy

Ultimately, a service strategy has to direct organizational actions that make it the first choice for its clients. Managers have to develop strategies which are directed at providing a working environment for all staff that mirrors the same spirit of service they aspire to for their paying clients. The title of Albrecht's later book, *The North-bound Train*, is a metaphor for achieving a focused vision for success and a direction for arriving there. Albrecht poses the question 'Which train are you going to ride?' as a challenge for readers to question their direction.[23] The service strategy is as much about providing meaning to energize staff as it is about delivering value to clients to retain their patronage.

Phase 3 is to educate the organization and is premised on a belief that:

3 Training and development of employees and communication are essential to creating and maintaining a service psyche

It is not enough to simply preach the gospel and 'walk the talk'; others have to be taught how to practise quality service. Continually backing up messages with explicit management commitment will ensure that all employees learn how to satisfy clients, internal or external, and how to be committed to successful service delivery rather than just doing a job.

In phase 4, the aim is to implement service improvements at the grassroots level. It is at this point that management has to:

4 *Empower employees with the discretion needed to manage the moments of truth of internal and external clients effectively*

The ownership of the initiative must be spread evenly throughout the organization and the pyramid of authority reversed to support the front-line staff with a facilitating leadership style. Communication, data and other organizational systems and structures should be re-aligned to support the client interface.

Finally, phase 5 suggests strategies to make service quality an enduring part of the organization. In the end:

5 *All of an organization's people, policies and systems should be aligned to creating exceptional value in the eyes of its clients*

Rather than each of the operations (e.g. delivery of courses, enrolments, research projects) being programmes with particular client service needs, providing quality service to ensure success becomes the way an organization conducts business, and should be indelibly etched into its culture. Incentive and recognition systems for staff become part of this mosaic to complete a continuous loop of service success.

Client service best practice checklist

The following checklist for best practice client service may be articulated with criteria used to judge those who apply for a range of quality awards which are discussed at the end of this chapter.

Client value focus
1 Identify clients who include all beneficiaries, internal and external.
2 Conduct regular and rigorous research, objective and subjective, to appreciate what contributes to beneficiary value in clients' perception.
3 Balance needs through mediation to maximize beneficiary value.

Service strategies and action planning
1 Realistic premises of value creation should be based on client research, and appraisal of the current status and the emerging environment, to provide meaning and direction.

2 The vision, mission and values must convey legitimate messages based on value creation strategies which beneficiaries can relate to, as well as support and endorse.

3 Planning must guide and align everyday actions towards achievement of client-focused goals.

Education, training and communication

1 Ensures awareness, develops service skills and uses quality improvement skills and tools, including understanding of the causes of variation, and client survey techniques which are qualitative and quantitative.

2 Encourages open and receptive communication designed to imbue a sense of community and shared meanings, shared values and shared knowledge that enhances the potential to create beneficiary value which can be transformed into reality.

3 Creates a learning organization that continually evaluates the roles it should play in creating superior beneficiary value.

Continuous process improvement

1 Considers all organizational processes as merely temporary solutions continually subject to review to improve their aim of delivering value.

2 Undertakes perpetual effort to make all processes client-friendly.

3 Ensures all processes within systems are improved continuously or re-engineered to maximize beneficiary value through better quality and/or productivity.

4 Encourages creativity and innovative ideas by acknowledging them formally and actively.

Empowerment

1 Is directed at all beneficiaries, but particularly front-line staff and their clients.

2 Gives freedom, embraces willingness and gives confidence to act competently, not recklessly.

3 Encourages partnering and the development of teams.

4 Facilitates active involvement of the workforce in planning.

Measurement, analysis and feedback

1 Are designed to support service strategies, not overpower them.

2 Provide a system that empowers the people who do the work to create value, not for control or to measure production at the expense of quality.

3 Include regular assessment of client satisfaction and priorities for improvement.

4 Support relative team efficiency and process efficiency using benchmarking and best practice which builds both a competitive spirit and the spirit of learning from each other.

Appreciation for quality improvement
1 Is assigned according to level of contribution rather than level in the organization.
2 Recognizes and celebrates quality improvements and desired behaviours.

Leadership
1 Is given in the spirit of service, not control.
2 Focuses attention on process and adding value rather than on hierarchy.
3 Provides a focus and frameworks for action (e.g. guiding principles, values), as well as clarity.
4 Mobilizes everyone, not just a few.
5 Provides accountability for, and overt commitment to, value creation, not task performance.

ISO 9000 standards

Origins of ISO standards

In Greek, *isos* is a term meaning uniform, homogeneous – equal – and ISO may be seen as a shortened version of this word.[24] Furthermore, it uses the letters of the acronym for the International Organisation for Standardisation (IOS) which was founded in 1946 to develop international standards.[25] In 1979, IOS launched Technical Committee 176 to look at generic quality principles in order that international, minimum standards for manufacturing companies could be established.[26] Such standards were meant to ensure uniformity and predictability of products: that is, reliability and quality control.[27]

Manufacturers in the USA, Canada and the UK have adopted the ISO 9000 series which was first published in 1987, and revised in 1994–5. The European Community (EC) entered a memorandum of understanding with the seven European Free Trade Association (EFTA) partners, Austria, Finland, Iceland, Liechtenstein, Norway, Sweden and Switzerland, in April 1990. In 1991, a further memorandum was signed to develop a single system for recognizing certification and registration bodies. The organization which was created is the European Accreditation of Certification (EAC), and comprises Belgium, Denmark, Ireland, the Netherlands, Germany, Greece, Italy, Portugal, Iceland, Norway, Sweden, Switzerland and the UK. The European Union (EU) and EFTA have bilateral association agreements with Poland, Hungary, Albania, the Baltic states, Bulgaria, Romania and the former Soviet states. Because there are national standards in Australia, China, India, Japan, Malaysia, New Zealand, Pakistan, the Philippines, Singapore, South Korea and Thailand, it is likely that future trade agreements in South-East Asia will include ISO 9000.[28]

The quality system management standards ISO 9000 were issued in 1987, and were based on already established British, Canadian and American standards, and some of the guidelines for the Deming Prize. Although ISO 9000 standards involve a system originally designed for manufacturing, they are being used to some extent in the education sector. It was noted by Barton that quality system standards do not prescribe the manner in which a system should be implemented in education and training.[29] There is no indication of what the educational content, processes, norms or performance indicators should be. These may be set externally by clients, government and professional bodies, or internally. However, they do specify what activities need to be controlled, measured and documented. Where applicable, competencies, performance indicators, standards and benchmarks are to be identified. Each organization will necessarily have its own focus, conceptual approach, creative processes, administrative structure and method of operation.

ISO 9000 standards clauses for education

Since 1994, the AS/NZS ISO 9000 series of standards have contained a quality improvement element, although this component and a client focus are generally not key factors in the application of such a standards system. In 1995 (approved April, published July), the ISO 9001 standards for education and training were issued.[30] Twelve of the 20 standards clauses are particularly relevant to education.[31] They are:

1 Management responsibility.
2 Quality system.
3 Contract review.
4 Design control.
6 Purchasing.
7 Purchaser-supplied product.
9 Process control.
13 Control of non-conforming product.
14 Corrective action.
16 Quality records.
17 Internal quality audits.
18 Training.

The other clauses are:

5 Documentation.
8 Product identification and traceability.
10 Inspection and testing.
11 Inspection, measuring and testing, equipment.
12 Inspection test status.
15 Handling, storage, packaging, preservation and delivery.
19 Servicing.
20 Statistical techniques.

Applicability to post-secondary education

The complex range of diverse activities which are involved in any academic programme in the post-secondary education sector do not favour the use of a quality system which has its base in the manufacturing sector. While it is possible to identify where infrastructure requirements are documented, and processes are being conducted according to the standards, shortcomings are readily evident in the academic areas where *academic freedom* sees little use of documentation of individual style and mode of delivery. A diagnostic audit conducted at Swinburne University of Technology, Victoria, Australia, in 1993 identified this dilemma.[32] The auditors found that at Swinburne, upper management procedures and responsibilities, which are often poorly defined in industry, were relatively well documented and in operation. The converse was found at the operational level. Suspicion, cynicism and apathy were cited as issues within the academic and service areas which need to be overcome when putting in place any quality management system.

Patten has emphasized the vital importance of diversity. In a highly emotive article in *The Times* newspaper in the UK, he declared that it is imperative that quality must be paramount, and that equal weight should be given to the many forms of excellence offered in a diversified higher education system.[33] Peace Lenn from the USA has pointed to three key elements in quality assurance in higher education. She believes they are accountability, common standards and third-party evaluation. It can be argued that the ISO 9001 standard for education and training provides these elements.[34]

Case studies undertaken at the University of Wolverhampton in the UK have been reported by Doherty.[35] They address clauses in the ISO 9001 standard related to procedures undertaken in the LLB (Hons) degree by distance learning and BEd and BEd (Hons) in-service degree for overseas students in order to illustrate that the ISO 9000

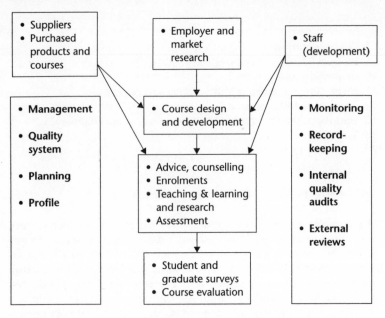

Figure 7.2 Areas of application of the ISO 9000 standards clauses in education.

series standards are applicable to higher education programmes. Doherty emphasizes that it is essential to understand that the international quality standard is about the management of quality, not just about systems which can be controlled whether they are delivering good or bad quality. He also highlights the difference between ISO 9001 and ISO 9002. The former comprises 20 clauses, which include two on design (clause 4) and servicing (clause 19), while the latter has 18 clauses, which focus on the delivery of a product or service. It is important that those wishing to meet the design clause are clear on the nature of the product or service. In the post-secondary education sector this relates to courses, research, consultancy services and the like. At the University of Wolverhampton the *product* is titled 'Learning Experiences' and attention is given to design control, design and development planning, design input, output, verification and changes. The university must demonstrate how it uses its strategic planning processes to deliver its mission, and must have its product standards verified by external experts.

Figure 7.2 presents the relationship between the areas of application of the clauses of the ISO 9000 standard for education. The over-arching necessity for management, an established profile, planning and a quality system on the one hand, and ongoing monitoring, record-keeping, internal and external audits and reviews on the other, is clearly indicated.

Jones has highlighted the challenge of transferring the language and concepts of the ISO quality standards to education courses at the Centre for Executive Education in Waikato, New Zealand. The Centre first achieved certification in 1994, with a successful review audit in 1997. Nevertheless, Jones indicates that a standards approach does not specifically encourage continuous improvement or creative deviation. Indeed, *standards encourage conformance and centralized bureaucratic management*.[36]

Meeting standards should ideally form part of a quality system which sees quality improvement as starting a chain reaction. Deming described the outcomes from quality improvement as a chain reaction involving improved productivity and the ability to stay in business. Deming's principles to achieve transformation include creating a constancy of purpose towards improvement, adopting leadership and responsibility as a philosophy, improving the system constantly, education and self-improvement.[37]

Key points in adopting an ISO 9000 standards approach

The ISO 9000 series standards applicable to the higher education sector in Australia and New Zealand are the AS/NZS 3905.5.1995 Quality System Guidelines, which are published as Part 5: ISO 9001: 1994 for Education and Training.[38] The quality system described can be put in place to:

1 Improve performance, productivity and coordination.
2 Identify objectives and focus on client expectations.
3 Achieve and maintain product and service quality (client needs).
4 Provide a baseline for continuous improvement.

There are four fundamental building blocks to an ISO 9000 quality system:

• the standards themselves;
• an interface between people and processes which is well documented to assure quality;
• a mission – the core purpose (not a set of targets or objectives);
• defined processes and systems.

The focus of ISO 9001 for education is on the management of the organization: the education institution as a whole. Therefore, it is most practical to make use of the existing structures, documents, procedures, methodology, forms and other tools in management that are already in place. A review will identify shortfalls and inadequacies. The documentation and practices should only be rewritten or replaced as absolutely necessary. ISO standards require an organization to manage and control all activities that impinge on its ability to provide quality services. For education, the curriculum and methods of delivery are not subject to regulation and control, beyond ensuring that outcomes are met, other than in some professional degree courses such as engineering.

In the post-secondary education sector, an ISO 9001 quality system should:

• be aligned to the educational environment;
• require careful interpretation of product and service in the academic environment;
• not require a further bureaucratic burden;
• incorporate only those processes critical to the outcome of services provided by the academic system.

The *product* or service in education may be defined as the provision of programmes and learning opportunities, knowledge and expertise to the needs of the client(s), e.g.:

1 enhancing an individual's knowledge, skills, understanding and attitude
2 the educational environment, curriculum, and resources
3 research output
4 community impact.

An ISO system does provide a framework to aid the development of flowcharts of management processes to ensure flexibility of the quality system chosen. It is not a means of setting competencies, setting or prescribing performance indicators, prescribing education content or processes.[39]

An example of transnational cooperation and the integration of TQM principles within a quality system using Australian Quality Awards (AQA) criteria, and resulting in certification to ISO 9000 standards, is presented to illustrate success. During 1992, the University of Southern Queensland in Australia began using TQM principles which were based on those used by Oregon State University and Colorado State University in the USA. A study of the relationship between the AQA criteria and ISO 9000 standards was undertaken for the purpose of identifying deficiencies in the management of documentation and processes.

In 1993 a report documenting the quality systems used at University of Southern Queensland (USQ) was presented.[40] It focused on five areas:

1 A quality benchmark.
2 A quality framework.
3 A structure for deriving and managing quality assurance policy and processes.
4 Potential fail points.
5 Recommendations.

A major feature of the recommendations was the need for individuals in all of USQ's divisions, departments and sections to take responsibility for quality. Adoption of the ISO 9000 standards for the systems in the university, and an approach based on the AQA criteria, to ensure a people focus, were put in place.

In November 1995, the Australian publication *Campus Review* reported that USQ's computing facilities provider, Information Technology Services (ITS), had won certification for successfully implementing a quality management system conforming with the ISO 9001 standard. The Vice-Chancellor, Professor Barry Leal, saw ISO certification as an achievement which would ensure that the services provided by ITS (computer conferencing, multimedia courses, on-line course materials provided through the Internet and video conferencing between groups of students and staff) were developed and implemented in a way which would ensure maximum benefit to students (clients).[41]

Relationships between ISO 9000 standards and other quality frameworks

There is a fundamental conflict between the philosophies underlying the AQA criteria, the model of programme and planning reviews described in Chapter 4 and the ISO 9001 standard. The last is, more or less, a prescriptive framework or set of guidelines for management process control, whereas the AQA criteria and programme and planning reviews are self-assessment tools. How is it philosophically possible to align ISO 9001 with either or both of these processes?[42]

A study was undertaken in early 1995 to align ISO 9001 criteria for education and training with the programme and planning reviews documentation used in one of Australia's larger universities.[43] Some of the recommendations made as a result of the study related to inconsistencies in documentation about commitment statements, communication strategies, organizational charts, job or role descriptions, resource allocation, designation of responsibilities to implement and maintain a quality system, an annual review mechanism and quality manuals.

It was concluded that the elements in clauses of the ISO 9000 standards which related to conformation of suppliers and purchasing processes and control of documents were areas not well considered in relation to education, and might be in conflict with principles, particularly in the higher education sector, which espouse the value of diversity and academic freedom. Nevertheless, any documentation of processes which are used to review operational units and their programmes against standards or principles using performance criteria could be aligned to the ISO 9001 standard as tightly as possible in order to minimize the workload of those who may choose to seek certification. Other recommendations from the study related to the need for existing work practices to be documented on flowcharts, with articulation of the sequence of activities undertaken in relation to a time frame (such as for enrolments, learning formats, assignments, examinations, graduations and all associated record-keeping).

Undertaking rigorous documentation provides additional benefits for new staff (and existing staff), students and internal or external auditors and reviewers, who can more readily identify the *who*, *what*, *how*, *why*, *when* and *which* of all processes and procedures, as well as ensuring the documentation is consistent and reliable. Where relevant, professional accreditation criteria can also be aligned to programme and planning reviews to avoid duplication and overlap wherever possible.

Robert Lundquist in Sweden conducted a survey on ISO 9000 in post-secondary institutions on a global basis in 1995.[44] He distributed 30 questionnaires to 12 higher education institutions and 18 at other levels of post-secondary education. Twenty-three replies were received and, of those, 18 had quality systems implemented, and one was considering implementation. Twelve had gained ISO 9002 certification, with most of these being achieved in 1993 (three), 1994 (four) and 1995 (three). Most (46.2 per cent) were in the UK or the rest of Europe (29.1 per cent). Involvement in the USA, Australia, New Zealand and the Far East ranged from 6.3 to 7.6 per cent.

To discover which (if any) universities in Australia were involved in undertaking ISO 9000 certification for any of their areas, a survey was conducted in Australia in the same year.[45] Contacts in each Australian university were approached to answer questions which related to:

- interest in ISO;
- areas of interest – academic or non-academic;
- progress towards ISO certification in ISO 9001 or 9002 in specific areas.

The results are interesting. In summary, 36 Australian universities were surveyed. Of the 35 which responded, 19 were involved in certification or progress towards certification in non-academic areas (such as printing services, information technology, enrolments, commercial and consultancy service areas), and two of these and six others were showing interest in academic areas such as continuing education courses. The remaining 11 universities indicated that they were not interested in using ISO 9000 as part of their quality management system. The university which did not respond to the survey indicated later that there was no activity at that time, although a group of students was undertaking a study of the commitment to ISO 9000 and/or other quality management systems in the higher education sector, which eventually produced similar results.

The survey was repeated in 1997, with little overall shift in involvement. There were 19 taking active steps, and 18 were considering certification. Of these, ten were teaching areas, mainly the delivery of short courses and continuing education, and 19 were non-teaching areas.[46]

ISO 9000: conclusion

A review of the literature and the outcomes from the global and Australian surveys suggest that currently there is little evidence of commitment to use of ISO 9000 standards for education in the higher education sector. Somewhat more interest is apparent in the vocational education and training sector, where competency-based standards often apply. Perhaps this is because there has been little experience of competitive pressure from the education market place. However, with an increasing focus on higher education, especially in the Asia–Western Pacific region, and particularly for Australia because of its position in the region, direct competition has become an issue. At this time, judgement of the offerings of post-secondary institutions may be limited to outcomes of quality audits conducted by the committees for quality assurance in education in many countries worldwide, reports in good universities guides and other league tables, and personal reports from recipients of courses delivered in a range of modes.[47] Should a move to mandatory standards such as ISO 9001 and other criteria (for example, those used in the AQA,

Baldrige Award and other quality prizes) be put in place, competition will increase.

Cycle time reduction (CTR)

Cycle time reduction was developed by Motorola University, and is a process improvement tool for *re-engineering* the way work processes are carried out to ensure they meet the needs of clients in the most efficient and effective manner possible. It is concerned with rethinking and comprehensively redesigning business processes with an aim to improving performance dramatically.[48]

The radical redesign of a business process impacts upon the culture of the organization and the way in which people work. The successful implementation of a redesigned business process requires the need for the change to be accepted by all involved. CTR is based upon two principles:

1 People cannot improve what they do not understand.
2 A successfully redesigned business process is one that is of value to the client.

It involves teams in process mapping, and by joining a CTR team participants are in the unique position of:

- viewing the chosen business process in its entirety as it is currently being conducted;
- identifying concerns or problems associated with the business process;
- developing a completely new business process.

As with all process improvement tools, there are guidelines of operation which should be observed, such as attending all the workshops (usually six days). CTR has two major expectations of the participants:

1 The chosen business process will be significantly redesigned.
2 The redesigned business process will be implemented within nine months and be self-resourcing.

In order to encourage the CTR team significantly to redesign the business process under review, the CTR workshop is divided into two phases – *as is* and *should be* – with three days being devoted to each component. There is usually a break of approximately three weeks between each phase to consult with co-workers.

As is phase

1 Describes the CTR process in greater detail.
2 Assists in developing a team environment.
3 Flowcharts the way the business process is currently being conducted.
4 Highlights and captures all the concerns, problems and weaknesses (issues) associated with the work process.

Typically, a business process evolves and expands with the evolution of the organization. Through this expansion a business process can become inefficient and ineffective, as amendments are added to the process to meet the needs of the changing organization.

During the *as is* phase, the CTR team is asked to identify the way the business process under review is conducted. This identification is represented in a flowchart. Through the use of a flowchart, all the issues that the participants experience with the business process are elicited, and an illustration of how the work process may have become cumbersome and inefficient is constructed. (A break of approximately three weeks is observed after the *as is* phase.)

Consultation phase

Team members consult widely among their co-workers to ensure that all issues with the business process are identified before the *should be* phase.

Should be phase

The team is invited to explore redesigning the business process with the aim of making it more efficient and effective in meeting its clients' needs. The following steps are undertaken:

1 Without discussing the ideas, the team brainstorms ways to improve and change the business process. The team members are encouraged to provide all and any ideas they may have, no matter how bizarre an idea may seem.
2 Team members prioritize the ideas as a means to providing a skeleton for the redesigned business process.
3 The redesigned business process is flowcharted based upon team consensus. This consensus is vital to the success of implementing the new process.
4 In conjunction with the flowcharting, strategies (actions) that need to be undertaken in order to implement the new process are

identified. The responsibility for coordinating each of these actions will be delegated among the team members.
5 The issues identified during the *as is* phase are reviewed to ensure they are resolved by the redesigned process or the actions.
6 An overall team leader is elected to coordinate the completion of the actions and to ensure the redesigned business process is implemented.

Critical success factors for CTR

1 Initially there must be recognition by management and staff of the need to redesign fundamentally a current process focusing on the efficient and effective delivery of outcomes.
2 Senior management's commitment to change, and empowerment of the participants in the CTR team, to create and effect change.
3 The CTR team participants' commitment to the change activities and implementation of action plans.
4 Appropriate representation of the process stakeholders and senior management on the CTR team.
5 Consultation between team participants and their work colleagues at all stages of the CTR activity.

Stages of CTR

1 Identify the critical business process to be examined and elicit the support of senior management.
2 Identify appropriate participants for the CTR team (20 to 22 participants) ensuring they are representative of the process stakeholders, senior management, academic and general staff.
3 Brief the participants, and prepare the materials and venue.
4 Identify the way the process currently operates. Identify all the issues, problems and concerns associated with the current process. Consult with co-workers to ensure all their issues are recorded.
5 Identify how things should be done.
6 Identify possibilities for fundamentally changing the process.
7 Given the possibilities, create a new process, ensuring that the changes can be implemented within nine months and are self-resourcing. Identify those actions required for implementing the new process and assign responsibility among the team participants for the action plans.
8 Identify an overall team leader responsible for coordinating the next phase (implementation and evaluation). As a team, regularly assess the progress of the action plans and reassess priorities

when necessary. Report tangible improvements to management, co-workers and clients. Evaluate the redesigned process after 18 months.

Benefits gained through CTR

1 A clear identification of the outcomes expected by the clients.
2 Improving the understanding of quality service, by identifying the steps within the process that are of value to clients of the process.
3 Reducing the time elapsed between the expression of need by the client and that need being met by the process.
4 Focusing those responsible for the process on meeting the needs of their clients in the most efficient and effective manner possible.
5 Reducing costs and increasing productivity.
6 Increasing awareness of the roles and responsibilities of all the other areas, thereby increasing effective teamwork within the education institution.

Quality awards criteria

The Deming Award in Japan, Malcolm Baldrige National Quality Award (MBNQA) in the USA, European Quality Award (EQA) and Australia Quality Award (AQA) all base their judgement of candidates (including industries, businesses, government agencies, education and training institutions) on similar criteria which underpin quality management:

1 Leadership.
2 Strategy, policy and planning.
3 Information and analysis.
4 People.
5 Customer and client focus.
6 Quality of process, product and service.
7 Organizational performance.

The AQA and MBNQA were first presented in 1988, and the EQA in 1992. Each of these awards, although they have come into being in response to different needs in different cultures, has total quality as its basis. The assessment criteria are couched in slightly different terms, and each has a slightly different focus. In all of them, the elements in the criteria are linked, each considers approaches and deployment as well as results, and they are geared to create greater efficiency and effectiveness in organizations, and a better client and customer focus.[49]

The balance of focus on results or outcomes is marginally different. The AQA criteria examine how performance criteria and measures are used; how they are linked to the organization's vision, mission and key objectives; and how benefit and value accrues for all stakeholders (customers and clients, shareholders, employees, the community at large, suppliers). *Company operational results* and *business and support service results* are examined, with less overall scrutiny of links to objectives and benefits, in the MBNQA, while the EQA more closely resembles the AQA under its criterion *business results (what the organization is achieving in relation to its planned business performance)*. The EQA is the only award to address specifically the use of physical resources, which is implied in the others.

The MBNQA first introduced a specific education award in 1995, and the EQA moved to include not-for-profit organizations in 1996 (already in place for the AQA since its inception). Effective approaches, good deployment and integration, improvement strategies and improving outcomes are expected in all the criteria for an organization to win one of these prestigious awards. It is beyond the scope of this text to provide details of the criteria and elements of the Awards, but the contact reference points are indicated.

In Chapter 8, proposals for future directions provide a summary of the transformations that have taken place in quality management over time. The deliberations are undertaken in the light of evidence that there is a global market which will see national economies replaced by global economies, and a new direction for industrial capitalism. In the complex environment that surrounds post-secondary education, whither the value of diversity? How will the diverse needs of a range of diverse people be met in the global transformation? These issues are addressed in Chapter 8 and questions will be raised to inform the debate on the impact of focusing on managing quality and standards in post-secondary education.

8

PULLING THE THREADS TOGETHER

Introduction

The purpose of this chapter is to illuminate the key aspects of all the preceding chapters. Emphasizing the importance of a client service focus and transformation to foster improvement, the key aspects are put in the context of management theory, because the book is about *managing* quality and standards in post-secondary education.

Future directions

Looking to the next millennium, while national borders and societies with national identities will remain and provide differentiation in the foreseeable future, a knowledge-based society will become a more common thread linking nations and people. Along with a global market will be a global workforce. A knowledge-based global economy requires knowledge-based citizens. The role post-secondary education will play can be readily imagined. Those institutions which have, or develop, reputations for understanding the needs of society and the importance of providing assistance to evolving nations in preparing their citizens for the global market will prosper and grow.

Knowledge workers, those who provide or support the provision of education and training, could become the largest group in the global workforce. The application of critical problem-solving, analytical skills and theoretical knowledge will be critical to the success of nations. National and international as well as transnational accountability will be expected. Those who pay for training and education services have an expectation that they will be provided at the highest levels of quality. The expectation is equally important whether purchasers are public or government agencies, private companies with share-holders, scholarship awarding bodies or private individuals (who may or may not take loans to cover their expenses). How the quality of education services is assessed remains an issue. Credibility of those who undertake accreditation, certification, quality assurance audits and other assessments of institutions, their programmes, resources (including staff), students and graduates must move into closer focus.

Can we perceive the transformation to be a paradigm shift in the interpretation of the concept of quality? The industrially constructed TQM tenets are giving way to the more socially constructed ones as the quality paradigm continues to shift its focus towards service requirements, with service being synonymous with the total value for clients. This unification of *quality* and *service* thinking is the philosophy behind Albrecht's TQS model described in Chapter 7. In the long term all organizations, including post-secondary education institutions, exist to serve. Managers must be concerned with the creation of client value, and convey this to all staff through the way they manage their most valuable asset.

It will be important for a transformation to be effected in the post-secondary education sector for managers to be careful to balance the *walk* (demonstrating quality management and service quality practices themselves) and the *talk*. The talk refers to an approach which emphasizes the development of awareness of service quality through education, training and communication and the development of a vision, values and legitimate strategies to provide focus. It assumes that all staff will heed the messages and start to apply them to achieve the desired outcomes using the desired behaviours. But this takes time, and sustaining interest and momentum can be difficult in the absence of tangible success. At the other extreme, the walk focuses attention on pilot projects that have a strong likelihood of generating early success. Completion of pilot projects is meant to work on the principle that success breeds success. However, because it concentrates change activities on only a small number of people, it can be too narrow to foster more widespread support or sustain momentum in the absence of the talk.[1]

Grounding and driving initiatives in quality management and service quality to facilitate a change in culture, staff attitudes and behaviour takes time and requires a certain type of leadership to achieve the transformation. The type of leadership required must be one which embodies the spirit of service, not control or domination. That is, good leaders provide a clear vision and encouragement to pursue that vision, through an enduring commitment to it, and recognition for work well done. The desired atmosphere is one of learning, encouragement and a collegial approach to helping each other.

It appears that old paradigms die hard, even when they no longer work. In the 1990s, the teachings of the quality gurus have attracted increasing criticism, not only from organizations that claim to have failed in a business sense despite pursuing quality improvement, but also from other quality improvement supporters. For example, Albrecht, who in *The Only Thing that Matters* indicated that the pre-1990s teachings of the Western quality gurus lacked the focus that the Japanese developed regarding the importance of internal and external stakeholders (customers), and of qualitative measurement techniques. He asserted that the gurus' teachings were more concerned with improving physical manufacturing processes than serving customers. Such assertions were not well received by some of the gurus and their disciples who had become steeped in the prevailing dogma.[2]

As statisticians, both Deming and Juran would easily observe that a focus on *customers* in Table 2.1, which presents the principles of five quality gurus, indicates a meagre 5 per cent of the combined management actions prescribed for a quality transformation. They would also find a very high correlation among the gurus' prescriptions. It is acknowledged that Juran's *quality planning road map* published in 1988 did indicate a respectful customer bias, at least in the planning stage of manufacturing a product.[3]

There are a number of intractable criticisms that have been identified in the implementation of quality management in education institutions. They relate to:

1 Difficulty in applying the client/customer metaphor.
2 Lack of support for those attempting to initiate and then sustain quality management reforms.
3 Tensions between quality reforms and managerial reforms that seek to improve responsiveness and accountability.
4 Perceived conflicts between the attitudes and behaviours promoted by quality reforms and traditional academic values, such as academic freedom.

Barzelay suggests that the customer and client metaphor can be viewed holistically or depending on working relationships.[4] At the level of relationships, both internal and external clients' expectations can be quite unambiguous. However, even relationships with similar clients might require differential treatments. Attention to the diverse needs of similar clients and the similar needs of a diverse group of clients creates further tensions. A proposal to involve clients, and thus

empower them in decision-making around their needs and expectations, requires the service provider to create the environment and
shape the interaction in ways that improve the quality of the service
delivery function. The interaction must be considered in terms of
the real experience of the client, which does not mean responding
to his or her whims. Barzelay views the client as a source of evidence
about the quality of a service, rather than an arbiter.

Changing the rules and procedures is a well-recognized path to
aligning an organization with its changing environment. This will
inevitably be more difficult as education institutions become more
transnationally focused, involving diverse groups of clients with
diverse learning styles and increasingly impersonal, technologically-
based delivery modes. The constant is change, and the continual
search for improvement is the *norm* in modern society. If individuals
fail to look ahead for opportunities, are not prepared to change old
ways and adapt to grasp them, then chances are they will not survive.
By changing the focus of management, education institutions, like
other organizations, can prove to their clients that they are better
than their competitors.

Interestingly, Swiss identified four reasons why *orthodox TQM* had
to be modified if it was to be effective.[5] His *reform TQM* bears more
than a passing resemblance to the quality service paradigm. Building
on this, Ingraham discussed five issues that drew out the troublesome
implications of adopting TQM.[6] Likewise, Ingstrup looked at the key
elements of *total quality* and the leadership challenges in adapting
these, as is the case for education institutions.[7] In the final analysis, all
agreed that TQM, however defined, can make a major contribution
in improving the quality of services when adapted to the various
needs of individual organizations which also require other management insights and approaches.

In the USA, companies using quality management strategies have
been found to achieve better employee relations, higher productivity,
greater customer satisfaction, increased market share and improved
profitability. A recent Federal Quality Institute report found that
involved and personalized leadership appeared to be the most important factor governing the success of quality transformation efforts. In
addition, organizations that had tailored quality practices to reflect
their cultural and structural make-up met with success.[8]

This should not be surprising. Too often educators treat clients
(e.g. students and service teaching recipients) like family, with an
arrogant insistence on knowing what is best for them. Furthermore,
relationships and loyalty may be taken for granted, and needs not
heard or, when they are heard, ignored. Therefore, post-secondary
education institutions must increasingly adopt other approaches that

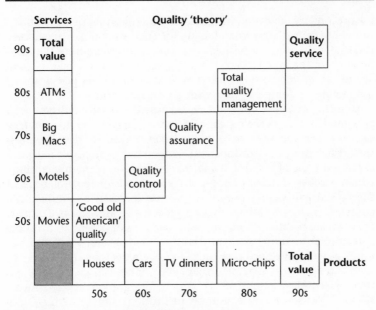

Figure 8.1: The changing quality paradigm
Source: Adapted from Albrecht (1992).

force them to reassess traditional relationships and focus on creating value to sustain them. It is a simple idea, to turn the emphasis from processes (traditional delivery models) and products (traditional courses and standard experiments or clinical experiences) to the clients and the services that they value. It is then possible to conceptualize the *quality service* ideology as the latest shift in the quality paradigm as presented in Figure 8.1.

Each successive shift should at least be cognizant of prior shifts as presented in an adaptation from Albrecht.[9] The quality *theory* can be applied to the post-secondary education sector as much as it has been to the manufacturing sector, although the relative importance of its various components may differ. As Albrecht points out, the further the journey progresses along the theoretical continuum, the more the axes tend to converge and the distinction between *products* and *services* becomes obsolete. They are interwoven when the client is judging quality. The way a course is delivered is seen to be as important as the standard of the course itself. Quality audits which do not equally attend to those elements are necessarily flawed. There can be no doubt that the satisfaction of the clients (students in this instance) will facilitate the marketing effort of a high-quality post-secondary education institution. Understanding the conception of quality as it is seen to add value for clients is the key to success. It has already been established that *value* is the creation of the combination of the tangible and the intangible experiences by the client at the various *moments of truth* that become his or her perception of interacting or doing business with an organization.

Albrecht, in *The Northbound Train,* provides details on the use of two models for preparing for the future.[10] These are the *strategic success model* and the *strategy formulation process*. He describes how they differ from conventional thinking about *strategic planning*, including the use of futuring. *Futuristics* is linked to scenario planning, which was described in Chapter 5. It transcends mere predictions of the crystal ball gazing variety to provide forecasts of future social contexts, including values, feelings, ideologies and so on. Futurists try to create pictures, trendlines and scenarios of potential, plausible and normative future societal states.[11] These are not predictions as much as well-developed constructs to inform decision-making. With such foresight, it is suggested that catastrophes can be avoided and that present-day actions are chosen to bring about desired future states.[12] Post-secondary education institutions should be involving futurists if they are to plan wisely in the global market.

Professor Stuart Cunningham led a project for the Department of Employment, Education, Training and Youth Affairs (DEETYA) in Australia titled 'New media and borderless education: a review of the convergence between global media networks and higher education provision', which made seven key recommendations. They were reported in *The Australian* newspaper in an article which highlighted fears of entry into the education market of large media and software companies. Australian universities were urged to position themselves by preparing to compete in the lifelong learning market. Government is recommended to develop coordinated regulatory frameworks for courses offered on the Internet. Accreditation and registration should be extended to these offerings, the report suggests. Maintaining a watching brief on the virtualization of universities, communication strategies and media networks was another recommendation. Further, the establishment of an 'Institute for Learning and Teaching in Higher Education' has been proposed to rationalize funding mechanisms for information technology to look at long-term goals rather than the current short-term approach. Two of the recommendations considered clients more particularly. These relate to putting in place robust consumer protection measures, with guidelines and regulations for borderless education, and an investigation of student demand for flexible delivery from a range of providers. Interest in the report has already been expressed in the USA and Europe.

The risk for transnational students who take education courses on the Internet is the homogenizing of course content of available offerings to the same extent that television soaps and chat shows provide populations worldwide with one view of cultural and community interactions. The involvement of GATE in the development of Principles for Transnational Education does not yet address this important point. Policies on interrelationships between post-secondary education institutions, telecommunications, information technology and the mass media must be developed across government portfolios, and globally across governments. Educationalists should be advisory to telecommunications bodies and vice versa. The field is wide open and the demand is high, particularly in the corporate sector. Education at any cost and in the shortest possible time frame via the most convenient medium provides fertile ground for those with profit on their mind. Attention to standards and quality of product and service will only be maintained as long as governments are prepared to insist on them in their own, and the ever-increasing numbers of private, providers. While all offerings must be regulated and accredited, whether they are offered via television, radio, the Internet, distance education packages or face-to-face, there will be protection for legitimate providers. Furthermore, perceptions of quality are likely to be based on interactions, so most of those who take education courses will want feedback, high-quality service and relevant programmes which will be useful in their daily lives at home, for future study and in the workplace.

The news is not all gloom and doom! However, the effect of a global market will be profound for those with special needs, such as women with young children, those with disabilities, the poor, those without access to technologies and those who have language difficulties in courses currently offered. The effects will vary, with some being positive and some negative. The ability to take up bridging programmes through courses on television without enrolling in them can empower people to enter formal programmes. Standards and quality are more easily maintained at a high level when those entering the post-secondary education sector are better prepared.

Whither diversity?

How can diversity be ensured when there is potential for thousands of students to enrol in a handful of courses that can be more easily, and often less expensively, offered via the Internet? Indeed, these are the sorts of courses that are being and will be offered. While there is global rhetoric about what is available, in most instances courses are taken locally or to some extent nationally. The diversity that is valued by clients will be best served by personal interactions to adjust courses and assessments to their needs. Heart-to-heart scholarly interchanges can take place on the Internet, but mentoring and other forms of support are more difficult. The choice of courses will be limited to the technology available, and practical experience will be more difficult to sponsor and support.

In this context, the idea is for education institutions to formulate value-creation strategies that keep pace with, or preferably exceed, the desires and preferences expressed in clients' value models, taking a reasonable account of emerging environmental factors and each institution's capacity for adaptation. In simple terms, the strategies to embrace are those that are rationales for success, provide organizational meaning and set the direction. As already indicated, Albrecht structures the meaning and direction into five levels, ultimately guiding everyday actions towards the achievement of client-focused goals in a number of key result areas.[13] At the heart of these strategies lies the definition and design of client-value packages, or service offerings, both tangible and intangible, that the institution provides in response to the truths it continually discovers from client research. These packages may be for diverse needs of diverse groups and offered for a range of delivery modes.

An interesting analogy for the dilemmas facing post-secondary education providers in a global and complex market can be found in the shifts between Frederick Taylor's (1911) *scientific management* and Elton Mayo's (1933) *human relations* schools of management thinking during the twentieth century.[14] It was not only the organization chart, distribution of functions and systems of work measurement that were important, but also the feelings, values, informal group norms and social backgrounds of employees that helped to determine organizational performance. Employees were recognized as people and not work units. However, the humanizing efforts then had to be tempered by market forces, since there is no point in having happy employees if you are out of the market.

The last word on managing

In summary, over time there have been many shifts and oscillations between the schools of management thinking. Managing quality and standards has been the focus in this text. Pollitt and Denhardt, among others, have summarized the evolution of traditional Western management practices to gain an understanding of the roots of managerialism. It is not necessary to repeat their work here. However, distinctive shifts in the management paradigm can be found that are similar to the changing quality paradigm shown in Figure 8.1. By renaming the axes to reflect what Pollitt refers to as *neo-Taylorism* and *human relations*, the general management paradigm would have shifted through a *decision and systems* phase in the 1950s, 1960s and early 1970s, to the *contingency theory* and *strategic planning* phases of the 1970s and early 1980s, to the *culture management* phase of the 1980s, which begot *managerialism* from the mid-1980s to the early 1990s.[15] Denhardt describes managerialism as being the application of market principles and business practices to management.[16]

This context of economic rationalism, under which managerialism was introduced, was later seen as being narrowly conceived and overly focused on minimizing costs or on immediate cost–benefit or other economic considerations, to the detriment of no less legitimate concerns, such as equality of access, responsiveness, social justice, probity, due process and service quality. It is these concerns that continue to be grappled with in the conceptualization of a more public sector management paradigm. Many post-secondary institutions are in the public sector, so the concerns apply to them. However, there is a consistency of view emerging in academic circles that public management cannot simply be derived by transferring private management techniques to the public sector, but from an articulation of general management theory that is sensitive to uniquely public concerns, such as accountability and the role of governments.[17]

In practice, managerialism has tended far more towards the neo-Taylorism axis than the human relations one. This has been manifested in greater cost-consciousness, significant staff reductions, a profusion of performance indicators and monetary incentives and extensive use of user-pays, contracting out and privatization initiatives. While this might have achieved greater efficiency in terms of the same or improved outputs for reduced inputs, there is little evidence of improvements to the effectiveness of outcomes or the quality of services. Often the approach taken has served to strengthen central controlling mechanisms, which means that any increased autonomy has been tightly constrained in a struggle to maintain basic services.[18]

In the past few years, however, there has been a resurgence of human relations management thinking. For example, the spirit of entrepreneurial approaches to managing the government's business, so successfully portrayed in Osborne and Gaebler's *Reinventing Government*, reignites the ideals of putting people and quality first.[19] This is reminiscent of the original vanguard of managerialism, namely the more generic prescriptions of cultural management put forward in Peters and Waterman's *In Search of Excellence* a decade earlier.[20]

To them, putting people first had two dimensions: respect for rank-and-file employees, particularly in relation to their development and empowerment; and closeness to the customer and client, involving commitment to listening and responding to their needs. These are arguably the most salient design issues for reforms in Anglo-tradition countries in the 1990s. In many respects this can be seen as a reaction to the excessive use of managerialism aimed at improving productivity and reducing costs, which itself was a response to the economic stresses of the 1980s. What is required now is a better balance between economic and social concerns,[21] particularly in the arena of quality assurance audits and accreditation processes.

This shift in the generic management paradigm takes us beyond managerialism or perhaps to a more advanced form of it. In much the same way as in the quality paradigm, the neo-Taylorism and human relations axes are tending to converge. Nowadays, there is also less of a distinction between private and public sector management approaches. As Professor Ian Saunders's research suggests, private sector managers are not as profit-minded as might be imagined.[22] Instead, they are relatively altruistic and attuned to social and environmental community concerns because these are integral parts of the quality mosaic. In this light, quality management focusing on service can be seen as an expression of the emerging generic management paradigm.

A shift in the management model is critical. To summarize the important requirements for embracing a shift in current models of management, Kotter proposes an eight-stage process for creating change:

1 Establish a sense of urgency.
2 Create a guiding coalition.
3 Develop a vision and strategy.
4 Communicate the change vision.
5 Empower broad-based action.
6 Generate short-term wins.
7 Consolidate gains and produce more change.
8 Anchor new approaches in the culture.[23]

Perhaps the most important change to embrace in post-secondary education is in transformation of the learning paradigm. Reflective practice in those who teach and a critical ability to move beyond established parameters and thinking in those who learn (in undergraduate courses, postgraduate research or continuing education for life) will naturally assure that quality is about improvement, not accountability. For the education sector, the importance of each institution addressing its own mission and goals when considering the quality of its curriculum design, teaching processes, student support procedures, research infrastructure support, postgraduate supervision, staff development programmes, reward processes, international interactions and support and equity programmes cannot be overemphasized.[24] The management of the quality of their courses, services and outcomes through evaluation and monitoring of feedback from students, staff, graduates, employers and alumni, benchmarking, internal and external networking and sharing of best practices, particularly in transformation learning, will enable institutions to demonstrate continuous improvement.

Shakespeare's *Hamlet* provides a closing gem on managing quality and standards in post-secondary education: 'Pray God, your voice, like a piece of uncurrent gold, be not cracked within the ring . . . we'll have a speech straight. Come, give us a taste of your quality'.[25]

APPENDIX: DEFINITION OF TERMS

accountability Exists where there is a direct authority relationship within which one party accounts to a person or body for the performance of tasks or functions conferred, or able to be conferred, by that person or body. A logical consequence of this is the application of rewards and sanctions when accountability mechanisms are activated. It is important to understand that this concept of accountability does not imply simply providing information or answering questions, but includes setting goals, providing and reporting on results and the visible consequences for getting things right or wrong. It also implies delegation of responsibility and authority, an essential element of which is that the delegator does not lose responsibility for performance and, therefore, depending on the circumstances, may be called to account. This definition enables a distinction to be made between accountability proper and other forms of activity which lack the direct authority relationship, but are sometimes referred to as involving accountability.

benchmarking A tool used to improve products, services or management processes by analysing the best practices of other companies or institutions (organizations) to determine standards or performance and how to achieve them in order to increase customer (client, stakeholder) satisfaction.

best practice The best way to do something. The concept can be applied at all levels of the organization, from the total management system down to individual functions. It is a changing concept as improved processes are integrated into the organization.

business process Organization of people, equipment, energy, procedures and material into measurable, value-added activities needed to produce a specified end result. Business processes are the administrative processes of the organization, including those that deliver a product or service, e.g. enrolments.

clients All those with a legitimate interest in the training system or individual training organizations. They include: customers (e.g. learners and enterprises); owners (e.g. governments and ministries, shareholders); funds providers and agencies (e.g. government departments of education and training, private investors); staff; sub-suppliers (e.g. child care centre contractors, business and industry for specialist lectures); regulatory bodies (e.g. training or regulatory boards with legislative requirements, accreditation councils and agencies); stakeholders (e.g. industry, professional associations, advocacy groups); the community.

continuous improvement Sometimes called 'constancy of purpose', this is a principle used by W. Edwards Deming to examine improvement of product and service. It involves searching unceasingly for ever-higher levels of quality by isolating sources of defects. It is called *kaizen* in Japan, where the goal is zero defects. Quality management and continuous improvement involves ongoing activity to seek constantly to improve the quality of process, product or service in the belief that performance can always be enhanced through incremental and breakthrough improvements.

critical success factors Elements and components in which results, if satisfactory, will ensure successful corporate performance. They are critical to the organization to ensure that it will meet its goals or objectives. Critical success factors are focused, fluctuate and are conducive to short-term plans.

cross-functional A term used to describe individuals from different business units or functions who are part of a team formed to solve problems, plan and develop solutions for process-related actions affecting the organization as a system.

customers The groups or individuals who directly use the products or services of any organization. Customers can be external or internal. For education providers, the external customers are principally learners and professional organizations or business enterprises. Internal customers are those who receive products (e.g. information, courses, research findings) and services (e.g. teaching, instruction, research supervision, consultancy) from other parts of the education or training system or those who share internal work relationships within the organization. It is not essential that any payment is made for a product or service for a recipient to be designated as a customer. Some organizations use the words client and customer interchangeably, while others differentiate *clients* as those who pay for a service or product or who receive a professional service.

cycle time The time taken to carry out a function from the beginning to the end. For example, the cycle time of project planning is the time taken from identification of the project to the commencement of the fully planned project. Cycle time is an important concept in continuous improvement and in some organizations the time taken to collect and analyse the data is often a major determinant in the total time cycle of a project. In manufacturing, it is calculated as the number of units of a work-in-process inventory divided by the number of units processed in a specific period. In order processing, it can be the time between receipt and delivery of an order. Overall cycle time can mean the time from concept of a new product or service until it is brought to market.

cycle time reduction Cycle time reduction, developed by Motorola University, is a tool for fundamentally redesigning the way work processes are carried out to ensure they meet the needs of clients in the most efficient and effective manner possible. It is about reviewing a work process that crosses more than two responsible areas, and identifying how interactions between these areas can be enhanced.

effectiveness The state of having produced a decided or desired effect; the state of achieving customer satisfaction.

efficiency A measure of performance that compares output production with cost or resource usage (as in number of units per employee per hour or per dollar).

indicators Benchmarks, targets, standards or other measures used to evaluate how well quality values and programmes are integrated.

inputs Products or services obtained from others (suppliers) in order to perform job tasks. Material or information required to complete the activities necessary for a specified end result.

international standards (ISO 9000) Describe the elements that quality systems should encompass but not how these elements should be designed or implemented. They will be influenced by the particular objectives, products, processes and individual practices of an organization.

kaizen See *continuous improvement*. The *kaizen* principle is continuing improvement in personal, home, social and working life.

key performance indicators (KPIs) The major indicators used by an organization or education institution to measure and demonstrate the extent to which its programmes are achieving the desired results indicated in its mission and goals or objectives.

measurable outcomes Specific results that determine, corporately, how well critical success factors and business objectives are being achieved. They are concrete, specific and measurable.

measurement The methods used to achieve and maintain conformance to customer requirements. Measurement determines the current status of the process and whether the process requires change or improvement.

mission The core purpose of being for an organization. Best expressed in the form of a statement no longer than 25 to 50 words.

operational plan Specific, actionable plan which, if carried out successfully, ensures that critical success factors are met, which in turn ensures that corporate business objectives are met. An operational plan is tied to critical success factors and contains detailed measures of success.

outputs The specified end result, materials, products or information provided to others (internal or external customers).

outcomes See *measurable outcomes*.

Pareto analysis (chart) A statistical method of measurement to identify the most important problems through different measuring scales (e.g. frequency and cost). Usually displayed by a bar graph that ranks causes of process variation by the degree of impact on quality (sometimes called the 80/20 rule).

performance indicators Indicators used by operational units, schools and departments to demonstrate the extent to which programmes are achieving the desired results. The three dimensions of programme performance (appropriateness, efficiency, effectiveness) need to be considered in context.

performance standard A goal or objective against which actual performance is measured.

process A particular method of doing something, generally involving a number of steps or operations. The organization of people, equipment, energy, procedures and material into the work activities needed to produce a specified end result (work product). A sequence of repeatable interrelated activities characterized as having specific measurable inputs, value-added activities and specific measurable outputs.

process improvement Enhancing the efficiency and effectiveness of those processes identified as critical to the success of provision of services, achievement of outcomes and overall impact.

process management The disciplined management approach of applying prevention methodologies to the implementation, improvement and change of work processes to achieve effectiveness, efficiency and adaptability. Critical to the success of process management is the concept of cross-functional focus.

quality The total effect of the features of a process, product or service on its performance, or on the customer's or client's perception of that performance. It is not just a feature of a finished product or service but involves a focus on internal processes and outputs and includes the reduction of waste and the improvement of productivity. In post-secondary education one single definition is problematic. Quality is related more to the relevance and value of each institution's mission, purpose, goals, objectives and the achievement of identified outcomes.

quality assessment The operational techniques and activities used to evaluate the quality of processes, practices, programmes and services.

quality assurance Part of quality management. It includes planned and systematic activities designed to ensure that clients are confident that the organization consistently delivers products and services of a high standard. The procedures used by an organization to standardize its core processes to ensure that its own output requirements and customers' expectations are consistently met.

quality audit Evaluation to verify the effectiveness of control. Includes the quality system, product and service quality, quality measurement, process-control practices and laboratory reliability testing assessments.

quality improvement Another key part of quality management which recognizes that achieving best practice is a continuous journey of improvement. It is a structured approach which involves staff throughout the organization using performance information to identify and act on opportunities for improving products, services and management processes in order to meet or exceed clients' expectations.

quality management The management of a process to maximize customer satisfaction at the lowest overall cost to the organization.

quality management system The collective plans, activities and events established to ensure that a product, process or service will satisfy given needs. The infrastructure supporting the operational process management and improvement methodology.

quality planning The process of developing the quality master to link together all the planning systems of the organization. The objective is to follow all areas of achievement of the vision, mission and business objective and to operationalize the strategy by identifying the requirements and performance indicators and the resources committed for these requirements.

quality standards Formally documented requirements, against which performance can be assessed. For example, quality standards for vocational education and training in Western Australia (WA) are statements of the characteristics or criteria which the WA Department of Training and the State Training Board have specified a training organization must meet to be recognized as a Quality Endorsed Training Organization (QETO).

quality system The organizational structure, processes and resources needed to implement quality management.

quality tool Instrument or technique that supports the activities of process quality management and improvement, e.g. benchmarking, cycle time reduction.

results Results are measures of how well corporate business objectives are being met. Results require that standards and goals for performance are set and the outputs and outcomes of processes and performance are tracked.

six-sigma A statistical term that indicates a defect level. One-sigma means 68 per cent of products are acceptable, three-sigma means 99.75 per cent and six-sigma means 99.999997 per cent, or 3.4 defects per million parts.

stakeholders Any persons, departments, organizations, agencies or bodies which have a clear interest in the outcomes of an activity. That is, they have an effect on the activity or are affected by it. Stakeholders may, on occasions, also be clients or customers, suppliers and/or partners.

standards See *quality standards* and *international standards (ISO)*. Formally documented requirements, against which performance can be assessed.

strategic quality planning Development of strategic and operational plans that incorporate quality as product or service differentiation, and as the load-bearing structure (framework) of the planning process. Includes: (a) definition of client requirements; (b) projections of the industry and competitive environment for identification of opportunities and risks; and (c) comparison of opportunities and risks against the organization's resources and capabilities.

targets Quantitative and qualitative in nature, targets usually include a date or time by when a stated outcome will be achieved.

total quality management (TQM) The application of quality principles to achieve the integration of all functions and processes of the organization. The ultimate goal is customer satisfaction. The way to achieve it is through continuous improvement. The creative involvement of everyone, from the chief executive down, in the continuous improvement of the organization's processes, products and services.

values All the things that are considered fundamentally important to the organization. These include what is strategically important as expressed in its purpose (mission), direction (vision) and key goals. They also include the basic beliefs of the organization and how they are translated into the behaviours considered essential to achieve the strategic goals.

vision The long-term future desired state of an organization, usually expressed in a 7- to 20-year time frame. Often included in the vision statement are the areas that the organization needs to care about in order to succeed. The vision should inspire and motivate.

NOTES

Chapter 1   Introduction: terms, principles and practices

1 M. P. Lenn (1997) The Global Alliance for Transnational Education (GATE): a new global organisation emerges. In *Proceedings, International Network for Quality Assurance Agencies in Higher Education (INQAAHE) Conference, 'Quality without Frontiers'*. Pretoria: Association Conference Organisers, pp. 109–12.
2 B. Ascher (1997) Is quality assurance in education consistent with international trade ageements? In *Proceedings of the INQAAHE Conference, 'Quality without Frontiers'*. Pretoria: Association Conference Organisers, pp. 1–9. P. J. Palin (1997) Human capital development and the role of GATE. *GATE Newsletter*, 2 (July), 14–15.
3 R. Lewis (1997) Why transnational education? *GATE Newsletter*, 1 (April), 8–9, at p. 8.
4 Ascher, *op. cit.*, n. 2.
5 Secretariate of the National Centre for Higher Education (1997) Principles for Transnational Education Courses. *GATE Newsletter*, 2 (July), 6–7.
6 European Association for International Education in cooperation with the Programme on Institutional Management in Higher Education of the Organisation for Economic Cooperation and Development and the Association of International Higher Education Administrators (1995) *Strategies of Internationalization of Higher Education: a Comparative Study of Australia, Canada, Europe and the United States of America*. Bonn: EAIE. Federal Ministry for Education, Science, Research and Technology (1997) *Comparative Study of Academic Credit Systems in an International Context*. Bonn: FMESRT. S. Algie (1998) A degree no longer guarantees a job. *Engineers Australia*, 70(1), 48–50. Higher Education Quality Council (1996) *Quality Assurance of Overseas Partnerships*. London: HEQC.

Chapter 2 Historical aspects of the quality debate

1 W. A. Shewhart (1931) *Economic Control of Quality of Manufactured Product.* New York: D. Van Nostrand.
2 W. Edwards Deming (1986) *Out of the Crisis.* Cambridge, MA: Massachusetts Institute of Technology Center for Advanced Engineering Study. A. V. Feigenbaum (1991) *Total Quality Control*, 3rd edn. New York: McGraw-Hill International Editions.
3 R. Zemke (1993) A bluffer's guide to TQM. *Training*, April, 7–16.
4 L. Dobyns and C. Crawford-Mason (1991) *Quality or Else: the Revolution in World Business.* Boston: Houghton Mifflin Co. A. Donabedian (1980) *Explorations in Quality Assessment and Monitoring. Volume 1: The Definition of Quality and Approaches to Its Assessment.* Ann Arbor, MI: Health Administration Press.
5 O. Port with J. Carey (1991) Quality: a field with roots that go back to the farm and questing for the best. *Business Week*, special issue, the Quality Imperative.
6 M. Imai (1986) *Kaizen: the Key to Japanese Competitive Success.* New York: Random House.
7 C. Morgan and S. Murgatroyd (1994) *Total Quality Management in the Public Sector: an International Perspective.* Buckingham: Open University Press.
8 Dobyns and Crawford-Mason, *op. cit.*, n. 4.
9 P. Crosby (1979) *Quality Is Free: the Art of Making Quality Certain.* New York: McGraw-Hill.
10 K. Albrecht (1992) *The Only Thing that Matters: Bringing the Power of the Customer into the Center of Your Business.* New York: Harper Business.
11 M. Barzelay with B. Armajani (1992) *Breaking through Bureaucracy: a New Vision for Managing in Government.* Berkeley: University of California Press. R. Denhardt (1993) *The Pursuit of Significance: Strategies for Managerial Success in Public Organizations.* Belmont, CA: Wadsworth. D. Osborne and T. Gaebler (1992) *Reinventing Government: How the Entrepreneurial Spirit Is Transforming the Public Sector.* Reading, MA: Addison-Wesley.
12 K. Albrecht (1988) *At America's Service: How Corporations Can Revolutionize the Way They Treat Their Customers.* Homewood, IL: Dow Jones-Irwin. K. Albrecht (1990) *Service Within: Solving the Middle Management Leadership Crisis.* Homewood, IL: Dow Jones-Irwin. Albrecht, *op. cit.*, n. 10. K. Albrecht (1994) *The Northbound Train: Finding the Purpose, Setting the Direction, Shaping the Destiny of Your Organization.* New York: American Management Association.
13 J. Barker (1992) *Future Edge: Discovering the New Paradigms of Success.* New York: William Morrow.
14 W. Edwards Deming (1994) *The New Economics for Industry, Government, Education*, 2nd edn. Cambridge, MA: Massachusetts Institute of Technology Center for Advanced Engineering Study, pp. 92, 123.
15 P. Senge (1990) *The Fifth Discipline: the Art and Practice of the Learning Organisation.* Sydney: Random House.
16 National Committee of Inquiry into Higher Education (The Dearing Report) (1997) *Higher Education in the Learning Society.* London: NCIHE.

R. West (1997) *Learning for Life (the West Report)*. Canberra: Australian Government Publishing Service and http://www.deetya.gov.au.

17 J. Brennan, P. deVries and R. Williams (1997) *Standards and Quality in Higher Education*. London: Jessica Kingsley. J. Kruithof and J. Ryall (1994) *The Quality Standards Handbook*. Melbourne: The Business Library, Information Australia. R. G. Lewis and D. H. Smith (1994) *Total Quality in Higher Education*. Delray Beach, FL: St Lucie Press.

18 D. D. Dill (1995) Through Deming's eyes: a cross-national analysis of quality assurance policies in higher education. *Quality in Higher Education*, 1(2), 95–110.

19 J. Baker (1997) Conflicting conceptions of quality – policy implications for tertiary education. Paper presented to the Tertiary Education in New Zealand Conference, May. T. Coady (1996) The very idea of a university. *Australian Quarterly*, 68(4), 49–62. J. Juran (1988) *Juran on Planning for Quality*. New York: Free Press. J. M. Steele (1996) Post-secondary assessment needs: implications for state policy. *Assessment Update*, 8(2), 29–38.

20 S. Goodlad (1995) *The Quest for Quality: Sixteen Forms of Heresy in Higher Education*. Buckingham: Society for Research in Higher Education and Open University Press.

21 R. Townsend (1970) *Up the Organisation. How to Stop the Company Stifling People and Strangling Profits*. London: Coronet Books.

Chapter 3   Quality assurance in post-secondary education: an international overview

1 M. Cardozo (1975) *The Accreditation Process, 1963–1973*. Washington, DC: Association of American Law Schools, p. 39.

2 L. Bram, R. Phillips and N. Dickey (eds) (1983) *Funk and Wagnalls New Encyclopedia*. New York: Rand McNally and Company.

3 E. Forbes, A. Knight and G. W. Turner (eds) (1986) *The Australian Oxford Mini Dictionary*. Melbourne: Oxford University Press.

4 H. C. Wyld (ed.) (1961) *The Universal English Dictionary*. London: Routledge and Kegan Paul.

5 C. L. Barnhart and R. K. Barnhart (eds) (1978) *The World Book Dictionary*. Chicago: Thorndike-Barnhart.

6 F. O. Pinkham (1952) The National Commission on Accrediting Progress Report. In *Proceedings of the Northwest Association of Secondary and Higher Schools*. Seattle: Northwest Association of Schools and Colleges, pp. 43–57.

7 K. E. Young (1983) The changing scope of accreditation. In K. E. Young, C. H. Chambers, H. R. Kells and Associates (eds) *Understanding Accreditation*. San Francisco: Jossey-Bass Publishers, p. 15.

8 *Ibid.*, p. 21, emphasis added.

9 G. Chernay (1989) *Accreditation and the Role of the Council on Postsecondary Accreditation*. Washington, DC: COPA Publication.

10 W. Selden and H. Porter (1977) *Accreditation: Its Purposes and Uses*. Washington, DC: COPA Publication.

11 Young, *op. cit.*, n. 7.

12 I. Birch and D. Smart (1989) Economic rationalism and the politics of education in Australia. *Politics of Education Association Yearbook 1989*, 137–51. D. Green (ed.) (1994) *What Is Quality in Higher Education?* Buckingham: Open University Press. M. Connelly (1997) The academic quality audit of an Asian postgraduate university. *Quality Assurance in Higher Education*, 5(1), 40–5.

13 R. Reitherman (1992) The forces behind accreditation. *Radiologic Technology*, 63(3), 203–4.

14 Council on Postsecondary Accreditation (1986) *Educational Quality and Accreditation*. Washington, DC: COPA Publication.

15 Council on Postsecondary Accreditation (1991) Accreditation. *The Quarterly Newsletter of COPA*, 1–6.

16 R. Glidden (1983) Specialised accreditation. In K. Young, C. Chambers, H. Kells and Associates (eds) *The Changing Scope of Accreditation*. San Francisco: Jossey-Bass Publishers, pp. 187–208.

17 Selden and Porter, *op. cit.*, n. 10.

18 Council on Postsecondary Accreditation, *op. cit.*, n. 15.

19 H. Kells (1983) Institutional rights and responsibilities. In K. Young, C. Chambers and H. Kells (eds) *Understanding Accreditation*. San Francisco: Jossey-Bass Publishers, pp. 107–18.

20 R. Kirkwood (1987) The myths of accreditation. *Educational Record*, 54, 211–15.

21 S. Dinham and L. Evans (1991) Assessment and accreditation in professional schools. *The Review of Higher Education*, 14(2), 217–37.

22 Reitherman, *op. cit.*, n. 13.

23 Birch and Smart, *op. cit.*, n. 12.

24 Barnhart and Barnhart, *op. cit.*, n. 5.

25 Forbes *et al.*, *op. cit.*, n. 3.

26 M. R. Jones (1993) Total quality management. In *Proceedings of the Australian Physiotherapy Association National Conference*. Melbourne: Australian Physiotherapy Association Publication, pp. 15–17.

27 C. J. Eastman (1992) Total quality management: the challenge for hospitals in the 1990s. *Medical Journal of Australia*, 157, 219–20.

28 T. R. Hadley and M. C. McGurrin (1988) Quality of care in state hospitals. *Hospital and Community Psychiatry*, 39(7), 739–42.

29 S. Livingstone and M. Zieky (1982) *Passing Scores: a Manual for Setting Standards. Performance on Educational and Occupational Tests*. Princeton, NJ: Educational Testing Service.

30 R. Thorndike (ed.) (1971) *Educational Measurement*, 2nd edn. Washington, DC: American Council on Education.

31 G. Glass (1978) Standards and criteria. *Journal of Educational Measurement*, 25(1), 57–65.

32 R. Mager (1984) *Preparing Instructional Objectives*, 2nd edn. Belmont, California: Pitman Learning Inc.

33 B. Bloom (1968) Learning for mastery. In Center for the Study of Evaluation of Instructional Programs, *Evaluation Comment*. Los Angeles: University of California, pp. 1–12. N. Popham (1973) *Criterion-referenced*

Measurement. Englewood Cliffs, NJ: Prentice Hall. R. Tyler (1973) Testing
for accountability. In A. Ornstein (ed.) *Accountability for Teachers and
School Administrators*. Belmont, CA: Feardon Publishers.

34 J. Meskauskas (1976) Evaluation models for criterion-referenced testing:
views regarding mastery and standards-setting. *Review of Educational
Research*, 46, 133–58.

35 R. Glaser (1963) Instructional technology and the measurement of learning outcomes: some questions. *American Psychologist*, 18, 519–21.

36 Glass, *op. cit.*, n. 31.

37 S. Myers (1990) Program evaluation for accreditation. *The American Journal
of Occupational Therapy*, 44(9), 823–6.

38 B. May (1977) Evaluation in a competency-based education system.
Physical Therapy, 57, 28–33. J. Beenhaker (1987) Determinants in physio-
therapy education. *Medical Teacher*, 9(2), 161–5. C. B. Liston (1993) *The
Relevance of Competency-based Standards to Higher Education Workbook I.
Competency-based Standards Project*. Perth: Curtin University of Technology
Publication.

39 M. Scriven (1978) How to anchor standards. *Journal of Educational Measurement*, 15(4), 273–5.

40 Glass, *op. cit.*, n. 31, p. 242.

41 J. Norcini, J. Shea and D. Kanya (1988) The effect of various factors on
standard setting. *Journal of Educational Measurement*, 25(1), 57–65.

42 R. Hall (1975) *Occupations and the Social Structure*, 2nd edn. Englewood
Cliffs, NJ: Prentice Hall.

43 M. Chidley and C. Kisner (1979) Systematic curricula development in
physical therapy. *Physical Therapy*, 59, 409–17. J. Nethery (1981) Physical
therapy competencies in clinical education. *Physical Therapy*, 61, 1442–
6. C. Ellingham and K. Fleischaker (1982) Competencies in physical
therapy. *Physical Therapy*, 62, 845–9.

44 Chidley and Kisner, *op. cit.*, n. 43.

45 R. Burns and J. Klingstedt (1973) *Competency-based Education. An Introduction*. Englewood Cliffs, NJ: Prentice Hall.

46 Nethery, *op. cit.*, n. 43. Ellingham and Fleischaker, *op. cit.*, n. 43.

47 C. Davis, M. Anderson and J. Jagger (1979) Competency: the what, why
and how of it. *Physical Therapy*, 59, 1088–94.

48 R. Rancourt and C. Ballantine (1990) An analysis of the epistemic orientation of first- and third-year students in a physiotherapy program.
Physiotherapy Canada, 42, 241–51.

49 B. Spivey (1971) A technique to determine curriculum content. *Journal
of Medical Education*, 46, 269–74.

50 M. Bullock (1988) The development of approaches to curriculum planning to meet academic and professional objectives. *The Australian Journal
of Physiotherapy*, 34(4), 203–8. K. Shepard and G. Jensen (1990) Physical
therapist curricula for the 1990s; educating the reflective practitioner.
Physical Therapy, 70, 566–73.

51 Rancourt and Ballantine, *op. cit.*, n. 48.

52 W. McGaghie *et al.* (1978) *Competency-based Curriculum Development in
Medical Education: an Introduction*. Geneva: World Health Organisation.

53 N. Burton (1978) Societal standards. *Journal of Educational Measurement*, 15(4), 263–71.

54 B. S. Bloom *et al.* (1956) *Taxonomy of Educational Objectives. Handbook 1: Cognitive Domain.* New York: David McKay.

55 R. Beard, F. Healy and P. Holloway (1974) *Objectives in Higher Education*, 2nd edn. London: Society for Research into Higher Education.

56 E. Locke and G. Latham (1990) *A Theory of Goal Setting and Task Performance.* Englewood Cliffs, NJ: Prentice Hall.

57 P. Jarvis (1983) *Professional Education.* London: Croom Helm.

58 Chernay, *op. cit.*, n. 9.

59 M. Pagliarulo (1986) Accreditation. Its nature, process and effective implementation. *Physical Therapy*, 66(7), 1114–18.

60 W. H. Bergquist (1995) *Quality through Access, Access with Quality.* San Francisco: Jossey-Bass Publishers. National Board of Employment Education and Training (1997) *International Perspectives on Selection Methods of Entry into Higher Education.* Commissioned report 57. Canberra: Australian Government Publishing Service.

61 S. Jaschik (1991) Education department accreditation panel thrust into midst of some of higher education's most volatile issues. *Chronicle of Higher Education*, 37(26), 21–2. H. Kells (1992) *Self-regulation in Higher Education: a Multinational Perspective on Collaborative Systems of Quality Assurance and Control.* Higher Education Policy Series 15. London: Jessica Kingsley. Connelly, *op. cit.*, n. 12. N. Jackson (1997) Internal academic quality audit in UK higher education: part II – implications for a national quality assurance framework. *Quality Assurance in Higher Education*, 5(1), 46–54.

62 M. P. Lenn (1997) The Global Alliance for Transnational Education (GATE): a new global organisation emerges. In *Proceedings of the INQAAHE Conference, 'Quality without Frontiers'.* Pretoria: Association Conference Organisers, pp. 109–12.

63 Association of Specialized Accrediting Bodies (1992) *Report on International Issues Affecting Specialized Accreditation II.* Washington, DC: COPA Publication, p. 2.

64 C. Liston, M. Bullock and J. Cole (1994) *Australian Physiotherapy Competency Standards.* Brisbane: Body Control Systems.

65 E. Aston-McCrimmon and F. Hamel (1983) Physical therapy competencies: a market study. *Physiotherapy Canada*, 35(2), 77–83. L. Hollands and B. Vanbergen (1987) Professional organisations of allied health – discipline assessments: a review of four disciplines. *Australian Clinical Review*, 24 (March), 36–40. P. Stevenin, F. Chambon and F. Ducros (1987) Analysis of the needs for training of physiotherapists in the year 2000. In *Proceedings of the World Confederation of Physical Therapy 10th International Congress.* Sydney: Australian Physiotherapy Association Publication, pp. 81–5.

66 W. Rheault and E. Shafernich-Coulson (1988) Relationship between academic achievement and clinical performance in a physical therapy education program. *Physical Therapy*, 68(3), 378–80.

67 B. Mansfield (1989) Competence and standards. In J. Burke (ed.) *Competency Based Education and Training.* London: The Falmer Press, pp. 26–38.

A. Gonczi, P. Hager and L. Oliver (1990) *Establishing Competency-based Standards in the Professions. National Office of Overseas Skills Recognition (NOOSR) Research Paper No. 1.* Canberra: Australian Government Publishing Service. G. Masters and D. McCurry (1990) *Competency-based Assessment in the Professions. National Office of Overseas Skills Recognition (NOOSR) Research Paper No. 2.* Canberra: Australian Government Publishing Service. C. B. Liston (1991) A comparative study of physiotherapy education standards. In *Proceedings of the World Confederation of Physical Therapy 11th International Congress.* London: Chartered Society of Physiotherapy, pp. 153–5. Liston *et al., op. cit.,* n. 64.

68 C. Leatherman (1991) Specialized accrediting agencies challenged by campus officials. *Chronicle of Higher Education,* 38(4), 1, 22.

69 E. O'Neil (1997) Using accreditation for your purposes. *American Association for Higher Education Bulletin,* 49(10), 10–13.

70 J. Kandor and C. Bobby (1991) Accreditation standards revision: democratic, unilateral or dictatorial. *Counsellor Education and Supervision,* 31, 22–31.

71 Barnhart and Barnhart, *op. cit.,* n. 5.

72 B. Shimberg (1982) *Occupational Licensing: a Public Perspective.* Princeton, NJ: Educational Testing Service.

73 M. Lunz (1991) Personal communication. Chicago: Board of Registry.

74 R. Berggren (1991) Institutional accreditation for graduate medical education. *Plastic and Reconstructive Surgery,* 88(6), 1093–8.

75 L. Loesch (1984) Professional credentialing in counselling. *Counselling and Human Development,* 17(2), 1–11.

76 A. I. Vroeijenstijn (1995) *Improvement and Accountability. Navigating between Scylla and Charybdis: Guide for External Quality Assurance in Higher Education.* Higher Education Policy Series 30. London: Jessica Kingsley.

77 Australian Medical Council (1992) *The Assessment and Accreditation of Medical Schools by the Australian Medical Council.* Queanbeyan: Better Printing Service.

78 P. Leathem (1991) Thirteen steps to outcomes accreditation: Maine West's experience. *North Central Association Quarterly,* 65(3), 470–5.

79 J. L. Green and J. C. Stone (1977) *Curriculum Evaluation Theory and Practice.* New York: Springer. R. M. Diamond (1989) *Designing and Improving Courses and Curricula in Higher Education. A Systematic Approach.* San Francisco: Jossey-Bass. W. M. K. Trochim (1996) Teaching evaluation. Criteria for accrediting graduate programs in evaluation. *Evaluation News and Comment,* 5(2), 54–7. D. S. Anderson (1990) Mere technicians? In D. S. Anderson (ed.) *The Undergraduate Curriculum. Educating Recruits to the Professions.* Canberra: Australian National University Printery, pp. 22–40. A. W. Astin (1991) *Assessment for Excellence.* American Council on Education. New York: Macmillan. Australian Vice-Chancellors' Committee (1992) *Guidelines for Quality Assurance in University Course Development and Review.* Canberra: AV-CC. G. P. Mullins and R. A. Cannon (1992) *Judging the Quality of Teaching.* DEET Report, Evaluation and Investigations Program. Canberra: Australian Government Publishing Service. D. Warren Piper (1993) *Quality Management in Universities, Vol. 1.*

DEET Higher Education Division, Evaluation and Investigations Program. Canberra: Australian Government Publishing Service. C. B. Liston (1994) The structure of educational accreditation. PhD thesis, Murdoch University, Perth, Australia. R. Aylett and K. Gregory (1996) The prospect. In R. Aylett and K. Gregory (eds) *Evaluating Teacher Quality in Higher Education.* San Francisco: Jossey-Bass, pp. 117–27. Connelly, *op. cit.,* n. 12.

80 Mullins and Cannon, *op. cit.,* n. 79.

81 D. Stufflebeam and W. Webster (1983) An analysis of alternative approaches to evaluation. In G. Madaus, M. Scriven and D. Stufflebeam (eds) *Evaluation Models: Viewpoints on Educational and Human Services Evaluation.* Boston: Kluwer-Nijhoff, pp. 23–44.

82 Liston, *op. cit.,* n. 79.

83 O'Neil, *op. cit.,* n. 69.

84 W. K. Selden (1959) The National Commission on Accrediting. In L. E. Blauch (ed.) *Accreditation in Higher Education.* Washington, DC: US Government Printing Office, pp. 22–8.

85 Young, *op. cit.,* n. 7.

86 Council on Postsecondary Accreditation (1989) *The COPA Handbook.* Washington, DC: COPA. A. Craft (1992) *Quality in Higher Education.* Proceedings of an International Conference. London: The Falmer Press. Lenn, *op. cit.,* n. 62.

87 R. Millard (1987) 'Relation of accreditation to the state and federal governments'. Washington, DC: Unpublished draft of speech.

88 Green, *op. cit.,* n. 12.

89 *Ibid.* D. Woodhouse (1995) *Audit Manual: Handbook for Institutions and Members of Audit Panels,* 2nd edn. Wellington: New Zealand Universities Academic Audit Unit.

90 National Committee of Inquiry into Higher Education (NCIHE) (1997) *Higher Education in the Learning Society* (the Dearing Report). London: NCIHE.

91 M. T. McVicar (1997) Developments in the English quality assurance system: rapid change and the move to the market. In *Proceedings of the INQAAHE Conference, 'Quality without Frontiers'.* Pretoria: Association Conference Organisers, pp. 133–6.

92 National Board of Employment, Education and Training; Higher Education Council (1997) *Quality Implementation and Reporting in Australian Higher Education.* Canberra: McMillan Publishing Group.

93 D. Illing (1997) New start in South Africa. In search of fairness and excellence. *The Australian Higher Education Supplement,* 14 May, 28.

94 J. L'Ecuyer (1997) Three years of evaluation in Quebec colleges. In *Proceedings of the INQAAHE Conference, 'Quality without Frontiers'.* Pretoria: Association Conference Organisers, pp. 103–4.

95 N. Begin-Heick (1997) Collaboration among universities in programme quality assurance: a case study of Ontario universities. In *'Quality without Frontiers',* pp. 23–6.

96 J. Lui and Y. Wang (1997) The first evaluation for graduate school in China. In *'Quality without Frontiers',* pp. 123–7. Z. Wang and M. Lin (1997) Research on quality assurance system of graduate education in China. In *ibid.,* pp. 207–10.

97 B. W. Imrie (1997) Professional development as quality assurance: now and Zen. In *'Quality without Frontiers'*, pp. 81–4. W. F. Massy and N. J. French (1997) Teaching and learning quality process review: a review of the Hong Kong programme. In *ibid.*, pp. 129–32.
98 A. A. Ashton (1997) External quality monitoring in the Caribbean. In *'Quality without Frontiers'*, pp. 11–16.
99 W. J. De Gast (1997) Quality assessment at a distance: the use of quality indicators in the DTOACP project. In *'Quality without Frontiers'*, pp. 49–54. D. Kristoffersen and C. Thune (1997) Cooperation in quality: the coming Network of European Quality Assurance Agencies in higher education. In *ibid.*, pp. 99–102.
100 T. Georgiev and W. Callaway (1997) New arrangements for the assurance of quality in Bulgarian higher education. In *'Quality without Frontiers'*, pp. 61–5.
101 M. Ostling (1997) Self-assessment for audit – a tool for institutional improvement? In *'Quality without Frontiers'*, pp. 183–6.
102 J. P. Th. Kalkwijk (1997) Sticks (and carrots) in external quality assurance in higher education in the Netherlands. In *'Quality without Frontiers'*, pp. 89–94. A. I. Vroeijenstijn (1997) Advantages and disadvantages of a comparative assessment. In *ibid.*, pp. 203–6.
103 D. Woodhouse (1997) Now what? The second (and subsequent) cycle of external quality review. In *'Quality without Frontiers'*, pp. 235–8.
104 L. Harvey (1997) Quality monitoring and transformative learning: changing international trends and future directions. In *'Quality without Frontiers'*, pp. 67–72.
105 P. M. Clark (1997) Quality and standards: the elusive yardsticks of higher education evaluation. In *'Quality without Frontiers'*, pp. 37–48. M. P. Horsburgh (1997) The impact of quality monitoring on the student experience: an international comparison. In *ibid.*, pp. 73–6. A. G. R. Male and A. Pollock (1997) Devolution and enhancement: quality trends in New Zealand and Scotland – a comparative analysis. In *ibid.*, pp. 187–90. P. Milton (1997) Quality assurance in English higher education. In *ibid.*, pp. 147–54. J. Newton (1997) Collaboration and partnership in the development and implementation of a quality assurance system. In *ibid.*, pp. 169–72. M. Yorke (1997) This way QA? *Quality Assurance in Education*, 5(2), 97–100.
106 T. S. Kuhn (1970) *The Structure of Scientific Revolutions*, 2nd edn. Chicago: University of Chicago Press.

Chapter 4   Quality improvement in education environments

1 W. Edwards Deming (1986) *Out of the Crisis*. Cambridge, MA: Massachusetts Institute of Technology Center for Advanced Engineering Study.
2 D. Billing (1996) Quality assurance for National Council for Vocational Qualifications (NVQs) in higher education. *Quality Assurance in Education*, 4(1), 5–11. Western Australian Department of Training (1995) *A Quality System for Vocational Education and Training in Western Australia*. Perth: TAFE, Technical Publications.

3 P. Cryer (1993) *Preparing for Quality Assessment and Audit. Establishing a Quality Assurance System in Higher Education.* Sheffield: Committee of Vice-Chancellors and Principals of the Universities of the UK, Staff Development Unit. D. Hickie and M. Sawkins (1996) Quality in industry and education: finding common ground. *Quality Assurance in Education*, 4(4), 4–8.

4 P. Dawson and G. Palmer (1995) *Quality Management. The Theory and Practice of Implementing Change.* Melbourne: Longman Australia. H. R. Kells (1995) Creating a culture of evaluation and self regulation in higher education organisations. *Total Quality Management*, 6(5/6), 457–67.

5 A. Ferguson (1994) The virtues and pitfalls of TQM. *Business Review Weekly*, 4 July.

6 M. Brassard and D. Ritter (1994) *The Memory Jogger.* Massachusetts: GOAL/ QPC Methuen. L. Glassop (1995) *The Road to Quality.* Erskineville, NSW: Prentice Hall Australia.

7 B. S. Bloom *et al.* (1956) *Taxonomy of Educational Objectives. Handbook 1: Cognitive Domain.* New York: David McKay.

8 *Ibid.* D. R. Krathwohl, B. S. Bloom and B. B. Masia (1964) *Taxonomy of Educational Objectives. Handbook 2: Affective Domain.* New York: David McKay. A. J. Harrow (1972) *A Taxonomy of the Psychomotor Domain.* New York: David McKay.

9 Australian Vice-Chancellors' Committee (1990) *Code of Practice for Maintaining and Monitoring Academic Quality and Standards in Higher Degrees.* Canberra: Australian Government Publishing Service. Australian Vice-Chancellors' Committee (1987) *Guidelines for Effective University Teaching.* Canberra: Australian Government Publishing Service. K. Ashcroft with L. Foreman-Peck (1995) *The Lecturer's Guide to Quality and Standards in Colleges and Universities.* London: The Falmer Press. Committee for Quality Assurance in Higher Education (1995) *A Report on Good Practice in Higher Education.* Canberra: Australian Government Publishing Service. C. Colling and L. Harvey (1995) Quality control, assurance and assessment – the link to continuous improvement. *Quality Assurance in Education*, 3(4), 30– 4. P. Tovey (1995a) Context specificity and quality continuing professional education. Part I: beyond the market. *Quality Assurance in Education*, 3(2), 32–8. P. Tovey (1995b) Context specificity and quality continuing professional education. Part II: towards a meaningful approach. *Quality Assurance in Education*, 3(3), 22–7. R. Withers (1995) Quality assessment: two traditions. *Quality Assurance in Education*, 3(2), 39–46.

10 G. Madaus, D. Stufflebeam and M. Scriven (1983) Programme evaluation: a historical overview. In G. Madaus, M. Scriven and D. Stufflebeam (eds) *Evaluation Models: Viewpoints on Educational and Human Services Evaluation.* Boston: Kluwer-Nijhoff, pp. 3–22. D. L. Stufflebeam and A. J. Shinkfield (1985) *Systematic Evaluation.* Boston: Kluwer-Nijhoff.

11 E. Grizzell (1960) Accreditation: secondary schools. In C. Harris (ed.) *Encyclopedia of Educational Research.* New York: Macmillan, pp. 15–19.

12 E. House (1980) *Evaluating with Validity.* Beverly Hills, CA: Sage.

13 E. Suchman (1967) *Evaluative Research: Principles and Practices in Public Service and Social Action Programs.* New York: Russell Sage Foundation.

14 R. Wolf (1979) *Evaluation in Education*. New York: Praeger.

15 R. Robinson (1984) Different approaches to the evaluation of programs and services. *Australian Psychologist*, 19, 147–60.

16 L. Cronbach (1963) Course improvement through evaluation. *Teachers College Record*, 64, 672–83. Madaus *et al., op. cit.*, n. 10.

17 M. Scriven (1973) Goal-free evaluation. In E. House (ed.) *School Evaluation: the Politics and Process*. Berkeley, CA: McCutchan, pp. 319–28.

18 R. E. Stake (1967) The countenance of educational evaluation. *Teachers College Record*, 68 (April), 523–40. R. Stake (1975a) *Evaluating the Arts in Education: a Responsive Approach*. Columbus, OH: Merrill. R. Stake (1975b) *Program Evaluation: Particularly Responsive Evaluation*. Occasional paper no. 5. Kalamazoo: Evaluation Center, Western Michigan University.

19 M. Partlett and D. Hamilton (1972) *Evaluation as Illumination: a New Approach to the Study of Innovatory Programs*. Occasional Paper, Centre for Research in the Educational Sciences, University of Edinburgh. M. Partlett and G. Dearden (1977) *Introduction to Illuminative Evaluation: Studies in Higher Education*. Santee, CA: Perfector Web Printing.

20 S. Kemmis (1982) Seven principles for programme evaluation in curriculum development and innovation. *Journal of Curriculum Studies*, 14, 221–40.

21 C. A. Sharp (1997a) Are theories of organisational learning necessary for evaluation? In *Proceedings, Australasian Evaluation Society International Conference, 'Papers to Evaluation: Equipping Communities and Government'*, Adelaide, October.

22 House, *op. cit.*, n. 12. D. Stufflebeam and W. Webster (1983) An analysis of alternative approaches to evaluation. In G. Madaus, M. Scriven and D. Stufflebeam (eds) *Evaluation Models: Viewpoints on Educational and Human Services Evaluation*. Boston: Kluwer-Nijhoff, pp. 23–44. Stake (1967) *op. cit.*, n. 18. C. A. Sharp (1997b) Goal attainment scaling in validation therapy for elderly disoriented people: an evaluation or a facilitation? In *Proceedings, Australasian Evaluation Society International Conference, 'Papers to Evaluation: Equipping Communities and Government'*, Adelaide, October.

23 Stufflebeam and Shinkfield, *op. cit.*, n. 10.

24 G. Glass (1980) Evaluation research. *Annual Review of Psychology*, 31, 211–28. Cronbach, *op. cit.*, n. 16.

25 Stake (1967) *op. cit.*, n. 18.

26 D. Stufflebeam *et al.* (1971) *Educational Evaluation and Decision Making*. Itasca, IL: Peacock.

27 Bloom *et al., op. cit.*, n. 7.

28 O. Ingstrup (1993) 'Total quality in the public sector', Notes for an Address to the 1993 Excellence Conference, Toronto, Canadian Centre for Management Development, 30 November.

29 T. Peters and R. Waterman Jr (1982) *In Search of Excellence*. New York: Harper and Row. D. Osborne and T. Gaebler (1992) *Reinventing Government: How the Entrepreneurial Spirit Is Transforming the Public Sector*. Reading, MA: Addison-Wesley.

30 D. Greising (1994) Quality: how to make it pay, cover story. *Business Week*, International Edition, 8 August.

31 V. Massaro (1995) Quality measurement in Australia: an assessment of the holistic approach. *Higher Education Management*, 7(1), 81–99. National Board of Employment, Education and Training (1994) *Costs and Quality in Resource-based Learning On- and Off-campus*. Commissioned report no. 33, October. Canberra: Australian Government Publishing Service. L. D. Weller (1995) The equity factor: a vital part of the quality equation. *Quality Assurance in Education*, 3(4), 44–50.

32 Ferguson, *op. cit.*, n. 5.

33 J. Strong (1994) Leading article in *The Australian Way*, July, 4.

34 Ferguson, *op. cit.*, n. 5.

35 C. Morgan and S. Murgatroyd (1994) *Total Quality Management in the Public Sector: an International Perspective*. Buckingham: Open University Press.

36 Deming, *op. cit.*, n. 1.

37 Australian Department of Finance (1994) Quality for our clients: improvements for the future. Discussion paper prepared by an Interdepartmental Service Quality Working Group. Canberra: Department of Finance.

38 E. Mayo (1933) *The Human Problems of an Industrial Civilization*. New York: Macmillan.

39 J. Clarke, B. Zimmer and R. Main (1997) Under-representation in Australian higher education by the socio-economically disadvantaged: review of trends and issues, and implications for university planning and practice. In *Proceedings of the Eighth International Conference of the Australasian Association for Institutional Research*, Adelaide, November.

40 P. Ingraham (1994) *Quality Management in Public Organizations: Prospects and Dilemmas*. Syracuse, NY: The Maxwell School of Citizenship and Public Affairs, Syracuse University.

Chapter 5   Linking quality management to planning

1 J. W. Walker (1992) *Human Resource Strategy*. New York: McGraw-Hill.

2 P. H. Meade (1995) Utilising the university as a learning organisation to facilitate quality improvement. *Quality in Higher Education*, 1(2), 111–21. P. Senge (1990) *The Fifth Discipline: the Art and Practice of the Learning Organisation*. Sydney: Random House. The Wider Quality Movement (1997) *Quality, Productivity and Competitiveness*. Perth: Standards Australia Publishing. G. Hamel and C. K. Prahalad (1991) *Strategic Intent in Strategic Planning: Selected Readings*. San Diego: Pfeiffer.

3 K. Ashcroft and L. Foreman-Peck (1996) Quality standards and the reflective tutor. *Quality Assurance in Education*, 4(4), 17–25. P. F. Drucker (1964) *Managing for Results*. London: Pan Books. P. Harmsworth (1998) Training for quality: fact or fantasy. *Campus Review*, 8(1), 6. P. H. Meade (1997a) *Challenges Facing Universities: Quality, Leadership and the Management of Change*. Dunedin: University of Otago. D. Warner and E. Crossthwaite (eds) (1996) *Human Resource Management in Higher Education*. Buckingham: Open University Press. I. Moses (1993) *Teaching Quality and Quality Learning in Professional Courses*. Canberra: Australian Government Publishing Service.

4 D. Warren Piper (1993) *Quality Management in Universities, Vol. 1*. Canberra: Australian Government Publishing Service, p. 18.
5 C. M. Down (1997) Commonsense, experience and nous. *Transfer. VET Research and Practice*, 2(1), 10–14. Mayer Committee (1992) *Putting General Education to Work: the Key Competencies Report*. Canberra: Australian Education Council and Ministers of Vocational Education, Employment and Training. W. Osmond (1998) ANTA queries West Review. *Campus Review*, 8(1), 5. I. Reid (1996) *Higher Education, or Education for Hire*. Rockhampton: Central Queensland University Press.
6 Y. C. Cheng and W. M. Tam (1997) Multi-models of quality in education. *Quality Assurance in Education*, 5(1), 22–31.
7 N. Jackson (1997a) Academic regulation in UK higher education. Part I: the concept of collaborative regulation. *Quality Assurance in Education*, 5(3), 120–35. N. Jackson (1997b) Academic regulation in UK higher education. Part II: typologies and frameworks for discourse and strategic change. *Quality Assurance in Education*, 5(3), 165–79. D. Kristoffersen and C. Thune (1997) Co-operation in quality: the coming network of European quality assurance agencies in higher education. In *Proceedings of the INQAAHE Conference, 'Quality without Frontiers'*. Pretoria: Association Conference Organisers, pp. 99–102.
8 Higher Education Quality Council (1994) *Learning from Audit*. London: HEQC. Higher Education Quality Council (1996) *Learning from Audit*. London: HEQC. Committee for Quality Assurance in Higher Education (1995) *A Report on Good Practice in Higher Education*. Canberra: Australian Government Publishing Service.
9 P. H. Meade (1997b) Leadership strategies for the implementation of recommendations arising from university audit. In *Proceedings of the INQAAHE Conference, 'Quality without Frontiers'*. Pretoria: Association Conference Organisers, pp. 137–42.

Chapter 6   Benchmarking and best practice

1 R. C. Camp (1995) *Business Process Benchmarking*. Milwaukee, WI: ASQC Quality Press. A. Evans (1994) *Benchmarking*. Melbourne: The Business Library.
2 S. Neville and S. French (1991) Clinical education: students' and clinical tutors' views. *Physiotherapy*, 77(5), 351–4.
3 J. P. McDonald, S. Smith, D. Turner, M. Finney and E. Barton (1993) *Graduation by Exhibition – Assessing Genuine Achievement*. Alexandria, VA: ASCD.
4 R. Liston (1994) *Graduate Student–Supervisor Relationships: a Review of Canadian University Policies and Regulations*. Ottawa: Canadian Graduate Council. I. Moses (1992) Good supervisory practice. In I. Moses (ed.) *Research Training and Supervision*. Proceedings of a conference sponsored by the Australian Vice-Chancellors' Committee and the National Board of Employment, Education and Training. Canberra: Australian Research Council, pp. 11–15. E. A. Holdaway, C. Deblois and I. S. Winchester (1995) *Organization and Administration of Graduate Programs*. Edmonton,

Canada: Department of Educational Policy Studies, University of Alberta. E. A. Holdaway, C. Deblois and I. S. Winchester (1995) Supervision of graduate students. *Canadian Journal of Higher Education*, 25, 1–29. R. G. Burgess (ed.) (1997) *Beyond the First Degree. Graduate Education, Lifelong Learning and Careers*. Buckingham: Society for Research in Higher Education and Open University Press.

5 G. P. Mullins and R. A. Cannon (1992) *Judging the Quality of Teaching*. Report to the Department of Employment, Education and Training (DEET) Evaluations and Investigations Program. Canberra: Australian Government Publishing Service. J. H. Finch, M. M. Helms and L. P. Ettkin (1997) Development and assessment of effective teaching: an integrative model for implementation in schools of business administration. *Quality Assurance in Education*, 5(3), 159–64.

6 J. O'Leary (1998) Degree standards to be set. *The Times*, 26 February, 9.

7 P. Chadwick (1995) Academic quality in TQM: issues in teaching and learning. *Quality Assurance in Education*, 3(2), 19–25. L. Harvey, S. Moon, V. Geall and R. Bower (1997) Graduates' work: organisational change and students' attributes. *Update* (Newsletter of The Centre for Research into Quality, University of Central England in Birmingham), 10 (April). Higher Education Quality Council (1997) *Assessment in Higher Education and the Role of 'Graduateness'*. Cheltenham: Distribution Department, UCAS. B. J. Ju (1997) Engineering accreditation and registration for professional engineers in China. *Society for Research into Higher Education International News*, 33 (January), 1–3.

8 P. H. Meade and R. J. Andrews (1995) Measuring employer satisfaction in higher education. *The Quality Magazine*, 52, 52–3.

9 J. Ainley and M. Long (1994) *The Course Experience Survey 1992 Graduates*. Canberra: Australian Government Publishing Service.

10 P. C. Candy, G. Crebert, and J. O'Leary (1994) *Developing Lifelong Learners through Undergraduate Education*. Commissioned report no. 28, National Board of Employment, Education and Training. Canberra: Australian Government Publishing Service.

11 L. Harvey (ed.) (1993) Employer views in higher education. In *Proceedings of the Second QHE 24-hour Seminar*, University of Warwick.

12 P. H. Meade (1996) Measuring graduate and employer satisfaction in higher education. In *Proceedings of the Eighth International Conference on Assessing Quality in Higher Education*, Queensland, July, p. 5.

13 C. B. Liston (1997) Results of a graduate attributes survey pilot. In *Proceedings of the Eighth International Conference, Australasian Association for Institutional Research*, Adelaide, November. C. B. Liston, M. Pickett and M. Gore (1998) Results of a graduate attributes survey (GAS) pilot. *Journal of the Australasian Association for Institutional Research*, in the press.

14 S. MacDonald (1998) Are firms going soft? *The Times*, 26 February, 2.

15 D. R. Witmer (1997) Does the extension of higher education to the masses degrade quality? *Society for Research into Higher Education International News*, 33 (January), 3–6.

16 National Committee of Inquiry into Higher Education (NCIHE) (1997) *Higher Education in the Learning Society* (the Dearing Report). London:

NCIHE. R. West (1997) *Learning for Life (the West Report)*. Canberra: Australian Government Publishing Service and http://www.deetya.gov.au.
17 G. Healy (1998) The future's global, and not so young. *The Australian*, 21 January, 35.
18 D. R. Witmer (1997) Is there a perfect quality assurance and evaluation scheme for higher education instruction? In *Proceedings of the INQAAHE Conference, 'Quality without frontiers'*. Pretoria: Association Conference Organisers, pp. 223–6.

Chapter 7   Models to consider

1 F. W. Taylor (1911) *The Principles of Scientific Management*. New York: Harper and Brothers.
2 K. Ishikawa and D. J. Lu (1985) *What Is Total Quality Control?* Englewood Cliffs, NJ: Prentice Hall.
3 A. Bolton (1995) A rose by any other name: TQM in higher education. *Quality Assurance in Education*, 3(2), 13–18. M. Clayton (1995) Encouraging a Kaizen approach to quality in a university. *Total Quality Management*, 6(5/6), 593–601. S. K. Ho and K. Wearn (1996) A higher education TQM excellence model: HETQMEX. *Quality Assurance in Education*, 4(2), 35–42. N. Indrus (1996) Towards TQM management in academia. *Quality Assurance in Education*, 4(3), 34–40. S. J. Sims and R. R. Sims (eds) (1995) *TQM in Higher Education. Is it Working? Why or Why Not?* Westport, CT: Praeger Publishers.
4 W. Edwards Deming (1986) *Out of the Crisis*. Cambridge, MA: Massachusetts Institute of Technology Center for Advanced Engineering Study.
5 W. Edwards Deming (1993) *The New Economics for Industry, Government, Education*. Cambridge, MA: Massachusetts Institute of Technology Center for Advanced Engineering Study.
6 J. Juran (1988) *Juran on Planning for Quality*. New York: Free Press.
7 C. Gronroos and E. Gummesson (1985) *Service Marketing: Nordic School Perspectives*. Stockholm: University of Stockholm.
8 W. Sasser, R. Olsen and D. Wyckoff (1978) *Management of Service Operations*. Boston: Allyn and Bacon.
9 E. Gummesson (1991) Service quality: a holistic view. In S. Brown, E. Gummesson, B. Edvardsson and B. Gustavsson (eds) *Service Quality: Multidisciplinary and Multinational Perspectives*. New York: Macmillan. K. Albrecht and R. Zemke (1985) *Service America! Doing Business in the New Economy*. Homewood, IL: Dow Jones-Irwin.
10 J. Carlzon (1987) *Moments of Truth*. Cambridge, MA: Ballinger.
11 Albrecht and Zemke, *op. cit.*, n. 9.
12 R. Normann (1984) *Service Management: Strategy and Leadership in Service Businesses*. New York: John Wiley & Sons.
13 C. Gronroos (1984) A service quality model and its marketing implications. *European Journal of Marketing*, 18(4), 36–44. A. Parasuraman, V. Zeithaml and L. Berry (1985) A conceptual model of service quality and its implications for future research. *Journal of Marketing*, 49 (Fall), 41–50.

A. Parasuraman, V. Zeithaml and L. Berry (1988) SERVQUAL: a multi-item scale for measuring consumer perceptions of service quality. *Journal of Retailing*, 64 (Spring), 21–40. A. Parasuraman, V. Zeithaml and L. Berry (1991) Understanding, measuring, and improving service quality: findings from a multiphase research program. In S. Brown, E. Gummesson, B. Edvardsson and B. Gustavsson (eds) *Service Quality: Multidisciplinary and Multinational Perspectives*. New York: Macmillan.

14 K. Albrecht (1988) *At America's Service: How Corporations Can Revolutionize the Way They Treat Their Customers*. Homewood, IL: Dow Jones-Irwin. K. Albrecht (1990) *Service Within: Solving the Middle Management Leadership Crisis*. Homewood, IL: Dow Jones-Irwin. K. Albrecht (1992) *The Only Thing that Matters: Bringing the Power of the Customer into the Center of Your Business*. New York: Harper Business. K. Albrecht (1994) *The Northbound Train: Finding the Purpose, Setting the Direction, Shaping the Destiny of Your Organisation*. New York: American Management Association.

15 L. Harvey (1995) Beyond TQM. *Quality in Higher Education*, 1(2), 123–46. F. M. Hill (1995) Managing service quality in higher education: the role of the student as primary customer. *Quality Assurance in Education*, 3(3), 10–21. M. Joseph and B. Joseph (1997) Service quality in education: a student perspective. *Quality Assurance in Education*, 5(1), 15–21. J. Rowley (1997) Beyond service quality in higher education and towards a service contract. *Quality Assurance in Education*, 5(1), 7–14. A. K. Sommerville (1996) Changing culture. *Quality Assurance in Education*, 4(1), 32–6.

16 Albrecht (1988) *op. cit.*, n. 14.

17 Albrecht (1990) *op. cit.*, n. 14.

18 Albrecht and Zemke, *op. cit.*, n. 9.

19 J. Barton and D. B. Mason (1991) *Service Quality: an Introduction*. Victoria, BC: Province of British Columbia. R. Denhardt (1993) *The Pursuit of Significance: Strategies for Managerial Success in Public Organizations*. Belmont, CA: Wadsworth.

20 Albrecht (1992) *op. cit.*, n. 14.

21 Albrecht and Zemke, *op. cit.*, n. 9.

22 Albrecht (1988) *op. cit.*, n. 14.

23 Albrecht (1994) *op. cit.*, n. 14.

24 E. Sprow (1992) Insights into ISO 9000. *Manufacturing Engineering*, September, 73.

25 J. R. Stewart, P. Mauch and F. Straka (1994) *The 90-day ISO Manual. The Basics*. Delray Beach, FL: St Lucie Press.

26 B. Rothery (1993) *ISO 9000*, 2nd edn. Aldershot: Gower Press.

27 B. L. Rowe (1995) ISO 9000 Standards and higher education. In *Proceedings of the Quality in Higher Education Conference*. Sydney: IIR Conferences.

28 R. W. Peach (1992) *ISO 9000 Handbook*. Arlington, VA: CEEM.

29 N. Barton (1994) Developing the quality system guidelines standard to ISO 9001 for the education and training industry. *Standards Australia Seminar*, Sydney, September.

30 Standards Australia/Standards New Zealand (1995) *Quality System Guidelines Part 5: Guide to AS/NZS ISO 9001 for Education and Training*. Homebush: Standards Australia.

31 R. Freeman and F. Voehl (1994) ISO 9000 in training and education: a view to the future. In R. G. Lewis and D. H. Smith (eds) *Total Quality in Higher Education*. Delray Beach, FL: St Lucie Press.

32 B. A. Calway and G. A. Murphy (1994) ISO 9000 diagnostic audit – use for tertiary education. In T. Banta *et al.* (eds) *Proceedings of the Sixth International Conference on Assessing Quality in Higher Education*. Hong Kong: City Polytechnic.

33 J. Patten (1993) Why degree of quality is essential. *The Times*, 6 December.

34 M. Peace Lenn (1993) Quality assurance in higher education in global tour of practice and resource. *Higher Education in Europe*, 18(3), 71–9.

35 G. D. Doherty (1994) Quality, quality assessment. Developing a BS 5750 Part 1 1987; ISO 9001 quality system and learning at a distance. In T. Banta *et al.* (eds) *Proceedings of the Sixth International Conference on Assessing Quality in Higher Education*. Hong Kong: City Polytechnic.

36 G. Jones (1995) Education and quality improvement: applying a standards approach to executive education. In *Proceedings of the AAIR Conference*, Perth, November, pp. 99–116.

37 Deming, *op. cit.*, n. 4.

38 Standards Australia/Standards New Zealand, *op. cit.*, n. 30.

39 C. B. Liston (1997) Can ISO 9000 work in higher education? In *Proceedings of the INQAAHE Conference, 'Quality without Frontiers'*. Pretoria: Association Conference Organizers, pp. 117–22. A. van der Wiele, B. G. Dale and A. R. T. Williams (1997) ISO 9000 series registration to total quality management: the transformation journey. *International Journal of Quality Science*, 2(4), 236–52.

40 N. Hughes (1995) Case study: how is the University of Southern Queensland using total quality management principles, the Australian Quality Awards Criteria, and ISO 9000 for continuous quality improvement? In *Proceedings of the Quality in Higher Education Conference*. Sydney: IIR Conferences.

41 Facility meets tough quality standard. *Campus Review*, 9–15 November 1995, 25.

42 Australian Quality Council (1995) ISO 9000. *The Quality Magazine*, 4(2), 18–22.

43 C. Liston, C. Allen, H. Chew, N. de Bussy and A. Lai (1995) ISO 9001 and program review project. Unpublished Graduate School of Business assignment, Curtin University of Technology, Perth.

44 R. Lundquist (1996) *Survey: ISO 9000 in Higher Education*. Sweden: Lulea University.

45 C. B. Liston (1995) ISO 9000 Survey of Australian universities. In *Proceedings of the AAIR Conference*, Perth, November.

46 Liston, *op. cit.*, n. 39.

47 L. C. Hattendorf (1996) Educational rankings in higher education: fact or fiction? *Paper presented at Eighth International Conference on Assessing Quality in Higher Education*, July, Gold Coast, Queensland. D. Ashenden and S. Milligan (1996) *The Good Universities Guide to Australian Universities, 1997 rev. edn*. Subiaco, Western Australia: Ashenden Milligan. J. B. Bear and M. P. Bear (1997) *Bear's Guide to Earning College Degrees Nontraditionally*.

Benicia, CA: C&B Publishing. D. Woodhouse (1997) Rankings and benchmarks. *New Zealand Education Review*, 15 (January), 7. D. Illing (1998) Scorecard takes guesswork out of university choice. *The Australian*, 14 January, 3.

48 M. Hammer and J. Champy (1994) *Re-engineering the Corporation: a Manifesto for Business Revolution*. London: Allen and Unwin.

49 Australian Quality Council (1998) *Australian Quality Awards (AQA) for Business Excellence*. St Leonards, New South Wales: Australian Quality Council. C. Mills (1995) *Comparing the Australian Quality Awards, the Baldrige Awards and the European Quality Award*. Sydney: Australian Quality Council.

Chapter 8   Pulling the threads together

1 F. Schmidt (1993) *A Blueprint for Launching Service Quality*. Victoria, BC: Ministry of Finance and Corporate Relations.

2 K. Albrecht (1992) *The Only Thing that Matters: Bringing the Power of the Customer into the Center of your Business*. New York: Harper Business.

3 J. Juran (1988) *Juran on Planning for Quality*. New York: Free Press.

4 M. Barzelay with B. Armajani (1992) *Breaking through Bureaucracy: a New Vision for Managing in Government*. Berkeley: University of California Press.

5 J. Swiss (1994) Adapting total quality management to government. In D. Rosenbloom, D. Goldman and P. Ingraham (eds) *Contemporary Public Administration*. New York: McGraw-Hill.

6 P. Ingraham (1994) *Quality Management in Public Organizations: Prospects and Dilemmas*. Syracuse, NY: The Maxwell School of Citizenship and Public Affairs, Syracuse University.

7 O. Ingstrup (1993) Total quality in the public sector. Notes for an address to the 1993 Excellence Conference, Toronto, Canadian Centre for Management Development, 30 November.

8 FQI (US Office of Personnel Management, Federal Quality Institute) (1991) *Federal Total Quality Management Handbook*. Washington, DC: FQI.

9 Albrecht, *op. cit.*, n. 2.

10 K. Albrecht (1994) *The Northbound Train: Finding the Purpose, Setting the Direction, Shaping the Destiny of Your Organization*. New York: American Management Association.

11 W. Dunn (1981) *Public Policy Analysis: an Introduction*. Englewood Cliffs, NJ: Prentice Hall.

12 R. Slaughter (1993) The science of the future, *Studying Futures*, 21C (November).

13 Albrecht, *op. cit.*, n. 10.

14 F. W. Taylor (1911) *The Principles of Scientific Management*. New York: Harper and Brothers. E. Mayo (1933) *The Human Problems of an Industrial Civilization*. New York: Macmillan.

15 C. Pollitt (1990) *Managerialism and the Public Services: the Anglo-American Experience*. Oxford: Basil Blackwell.

16 R. Denhardt (1993) *The Pursuit of Significance: Strategies for Managerial Success in Public Organizations*. Belmont, CA: Wadsworth.

17 G. Allison (1982) Public and private management: are they fundamentally alike in all unimportant respects? In F. S. Lane (ed.) *Current Issues in
Public Administration*. New York: St Martin's Press. Barzelay with Armajani,
op. cit., n. 4. Denhardt, *op. cit.*, n. 16. J. Dilulio Jr (1989) Recovering the
public management variable: lessons from schools, prisons, armies. *Public
Administration Review*, 49(2), 127–33. N. Hughes (1995) Public management or public administration. *Australian Journal of Public Administration*,
51(3) 1–23: 4 April, m754. Pollitt, *op. cit.*, n. 15. J. Stewart and M. Clarke
(1987) The public service orientation: issues and dilemmas. *Public Administration*, 65(2), 161–77. C. Ventriss (1989) Towards a public philosophy
of public administration: a civic perspective of the public. *Public Administration Review*, 49(2), 173–9.

18 Pollitt, *op. cit.*, n. 15.

19 D. Osborne and T. Gaebler (1992) *Reinventing Government: How the Entrepreneurial Spirit Is Transforming the Public Sector*. Reading, MA: Addison-
Wesley.

20 T. Peters and R. Waterman Jr (1982) *In Search of Excellence*. New York:
Harper & Row.

21 A. Yeatman (1987) The concept of public management and the Australian state in the 1990s. *Australian Journal of Public Administration*, 46(4),
339–53.

22 I. Saunders and A. Preston (1994) A model and a research agenda for total
quality management. *Total Quality Management*, 5(4), 185–202.

23 J. P. Kotter (1995) Leading change: why transformation efforts fail. *Harvard
Business Review*, 73(2), 59–67.

24 G. Gordon (1995) Higher education 2005: pointers, possibilities, pitfalls,
principles. *Quality Assurance in Education*, 3(4), 21–9. L. Harvey and P. T.
Knight (1996) *Transforming Higher Education*. Buckingham: Society for
Research in Higher Education and Open University Press. R. King (1995)
What is higher education for? Strategic dilemmas for the 21st century.
Quality Assurance in Education, 3(4), 14–20. G. Holmes (1997) Rethinking
universities: quality issues for 2020. Unpublished paper distributed at
GATE conference, Washington, DC, October. L. V. Meek and F. Q. Wood
(1997) *Higher Education Governance and Management. An Australian Study*.
DEETYA Evaluations and Investigations Program, Higher Education Division. Canberra: Australian Government Publishing Service. D. R. Witmer
(1997) Is there a perfect quality assurance and evaluation scheme for
higher education instruction? In *Proceedings of the INQAAHE Conference,
'Quality without Frontiers'*. Pretoria: Association Conference Organisers,
pp. 223–6. C. B. Liston and D. R. Witmer (1998) Students in transnational
education. Paper and workshop presented to the 17th International Seminar on Staff and Educational Development, University of Scranton, PA,
USA, June; and the tenth International Conference on Assessing Quality
in Higher Education, Penang, Malaysia, July.

25 W. J. Craig (ed.) (1955) *Hamlet*. In *The Complete Works of William Shakespeare*. London: Oxford University Press, Act II, Scene II, lines 456–61,
p. 884.

BIBLIOGRAPHY

Significant texts

Albrecht, K. (1988) *At America's Service. How Corporations Can Revolutionize the Way They Treat Their Customers*. Homewood, IL: Dow Jones-Irwin.

Albrecht, K. (1990) *Service Within. Solving the Middle Management Leadership Crisis*. Homewood, IL: Dow Jones-Irwin.

Albrecht, K. (1992) *The Only Thing that Matters. Bringing the Power of the Customer into the Center of your Business*. New York: Harper Business.

Albrecht, K. (1994) *The Northbound Train. Finding the Purpose, Setting the Direction, Shaping the Destiny of Your Organization*. New York: American Management Association.

Albrecht, K. and Zemke, R. (1985) *Service America! Doing Business in the New Economy*. Homewood, IL: Dow Jones-Irwin.

Ashcroft, K. with Foreman-Peck, L. (1995) *The Lecturer's Guide to Quality and Standards in Colleges and Universities*. London: The Falmer Press.

Ashenden, D. and Milligan, S. (1996) *The Good Universities Guide to Australian Universities*, rev. edn. Subiaco, Western Australia: Ashenden Milligan.

Association of Specialized Accrediting Bodies (1992) *Report on International Issues Affecting Specialized Accreditation II*. Washington, DC: COPA Publication.

Astin, A. W. (1991) *Assessment for Excellence*. New York: American Council on Education and Macmillan.

Australian Vice-Chancellors' Committee (1987) *Guidelines for Effective University Teaching*. Canberra: Australian Government Publishing Service.

Australian Vice-Chancellors' Committee (1990) *Code of Practice for Maintaining and Monitoring Academic Quality and Standards in Higher Degrees*. Canberra: Australian Government Publishing Service.

Australian Vice-Chancellors' Committee (1992) *Guidelines for Quality Assurance in University Course Development and Review*. Canberra: AVCC Publication.

Aylett, R. and Gregory, K. (eds) (1996) *Evaluating Teacher Quality in Higher Education*. San Francisco: Jossey-Bass Publishers.

Barker, J. (1992) *Future Edge. Discovering the New Paradigms of Success*. New York: William Morrow.

Barton, J. and Mason, D. B. (1991) *Service Quality: an Introduction*. Victoria: Province of British Columbia.

Barzelay, M. with Armajani, B. (1992) *Breaking through Bureaucracy: a New Vision for Managing in Government*. Berkeley: University of California Press.

Bear, J. B. and Bear, M. P. (1997) *Bear's Guide to Earning College Degrees Nontraditionally*. Benicia, CA: C&B Publishing.

Bergquist, W. H. (1995) *Quality through Access, Access with Quality*. San Francisco: Jossey-Bass Publishers.

Blauch, L. E. (ed.) (1959) *Accreditation in Higher Education*. Washington, DC: US Government Printing Office.

Bloom, B. S. *et al.* (1956) *Taxonomy of Educational Objectives. Handbook 1: Cognitive Domain*. New York: David McKay Company.

Brassard, M. and Ritter, D. (1994) *The Memory Jogger*. Massachusetts: GOAL/QPC Methuen.

Brennan, J., deVries, P. and Williams, R. (1997) *Standards and Quality in Higher Education*. London: Jessica Kingsley.

Brown, S., Gummesson, E., Edvardsson, B. and Gustavsson, B. (eds) (1991) *Service Quality: Multidisciplinary and Multinational Perspectives*. New York: Macmillan.

Burgess, R. G. (ed.) (1997) *Beyond the First Degree. Graduate Education, Lifelong Learning and Careers*. Buckingham: Society for Research in Higher Education and Open University Press.

Burke, J. (ed.) (1989) *Competency Based Education and Training*. London: The Falmer Press.

Camp, R. C. (1995) *Business Process Benchmarking*. Milwaukee, WI: ASQC Quality Press.

Carlzon, J. (1987) *Moments of Truth*. Cambridge, MA: Ballinger.

Committee for Quality Assurance in Higher Education (1995) *A Report on Good Practice in Higher Education*. Canberra: Australian Government Publishing Service.

Crosby, P. (1979) *Quality Is Free: the Art of Making Quality Certain*. New York: McGraw-Hill.

Cryer, P. (1993) *Preparing for Quality Assessment and Audit. Establishing a Quality Assurance System in Higher Education*. Sheffield: Committee of Vice-Chancellors and Principals of the Universities of the UK, Staff Development Unit.

Dawson, P. and Palmer, G. (1995) *Quality Management. The Theory and Practice of Implementing Change*. Melbourne: Longman Australia.

Deming, W. E. (1986) *Out of the Crisis*. Cambridge, MA: Massachusetts Institute of Technology Center for Advanced Engineering Study.

Deming, W. E. (1993) *The New Economics for Industry, Government, Education*. Cambridge, MA: Massachusetts Institute of Technology Center for Advanced Engineering Study.

Denhardt, R. (1993) *The Pursuit of Significance: Strategies for Managerial Success in Public Organizations*. Belmont, CA: Wadsworth.

Diamond, R. M. (1989) *Designing and Improving Courses and Curricula in Higher Education. A Systematic Approach*. San Francisco: Jossey-Bass.

Donabedian, A. (1980) *Explorations in Quality Assessment and Monitoring. Volume 1: The Definition of Quality and Approaches to Its Assessment*. Ann Arbor, MI: Health Administration Press.

Drucker, P. F. (1964) *Managing for Results*. London: Pan Books.

Dunn, W. (1981) *Public Policy Analysis. An Introduction*. Englewood Cliffs, NJ: Prentice Hall.

European Association for International Education in cooperation with the Programme on Institutional Management in Higher Education of the Organisation for Economic Cooperation and Development and the Association of International Higher Education Administrators (1995) *Strategies of Internationalization of Higher Education: a Comparative Study of Australia, Canada, Europe and the United States of America*. Bonn: EAJE.

Evans, A. (1994) *Benchmarking*. Melbourne: The Business Library.

Feigenbaum, A. V. (1991) *Total Quality Control*, 3rd edn. New York: McGraw-Hill.

Glassop, L. (1995) *The Road to Quality*. Erskineville, NSW: Prentice Hall Australia.

Goodlad, S. (1995) *The Quest for Quality: Sixteen Forms of Heresy in Higher Education*. Buckingham: Society for Research in Higher Education and Open University Press.

Green, D. (ed.) (1994) *What Is Quality in Higher Education?* Buckingham: Open University Press.

Green, J. L. and Stone, J. C. (1977) *Curriculum Evaluation Theory and Practice*. New York: Springer.

Hamel, G. and Prahalad, C. K. (1991) *Strategic Intent in Strategic Planning: Selected Readings*. San Diego, CA: Pfeiffer.

Hammer, M. and Champy, J. (1994) *Re-engineering the Corporation: a Manifesto for Business Revolution*. London: Allen and Unwin.

Harris, C. (ed.) (1960) *Encyclopedia of Educational Research*. New York: Macmillan.

Harrow, A. J. (1972) *A Taxonomy of the Psychomotor Domain*. New York: David McKay.

Higher Education Quality Council (1994, 1996) *Learning from Audit*. London: HEQC Publications.

Higher Education Quality Council (1996) *Quality Assurance of Overseas Partnerships*. London: HEQC.

Higher Education Quality Council (1997) *Assessment in Higher Education and the Role of 'Graduateness'*. Cheltenham: Distribution Department, UCAS.

House, E. (ed.) (1973) *School Evaluation: the Politics and Process*. Berkeley, CA: McCutchan.

House, E. (1980) *Evaluating with Validity*. Beverly Hills, CA: Sage.

Imai, M. (1986) *Kaizen: the Key to Japanese Competitive Success*. New York: Random House.

Ingraham, P. (1994) *Quality Management in Public Organizations: Prospects and Dilemmas*. Syracuse, NY: The Maxwell School of Citizenship and Public Affairs, Syracuse University.

Ishikawa, K. and Lu, D. J. (1985) *What Is Total Quality Control?* Englewood Cliffs, NJ: Prentice Hall.

Juran, J. (1988) *Juran on Planning for Quality*. New York: Free Press.

Kells, H. (1992) *Self-regulation in Higher Education. A Multinational Perspective on Collaborative Systems of Quality Assurance and Control.* Higher Education Policy Series 15. London: Jessica Kingsley.

Kotter, J. P. (1995) Leading change: why transformation efforts fail. *Harvard Business Review,* 73(2), 59–67.

Krathwohl, D. R., Bloom, B. S. and Masia, B. B. (1964) *Taxonomy of Educational Objectives. Handbook 2: Affective Domain.* New York: David McKay.

Kruithof, J. and Ryall, J. (1994) *The Quality Standards Handbook.* Melbourne: The Business Library, Information Australia.

Kuhn, T. S. (1970) *The Structure of Scientific Revolutions,* 2nd edn. Chicago, IL: University of Chicago Press.

Lewis, R. G. and Smith, D. H. (1994) *Total Quality in Higher Education.* Delray Beach, FL: St Lucie Press.

Liston, C. B. (1994) The structure of educational accreditation. PhD thesis, Murdoch University, Perth, Western Australia.

Madaus, G., Scriven, M. and Stufflebeam, D. (eds) (1983) *Evaluation Models: Viewpoints on Educational and Human Services Evaluation.* Boston: Kluwer-Nijhoff.

Mayer Committee (1992) *Putting General Education to Work: the Key Competencies Report.* Canberra: Australian Education Council and Ministers of Vocational Education, Employment and Training.

Mayo, E. (1933) *The Human Problems of an Industrial Civilization.* New York: Macmillan.

Meade, P. H. (1997) *Challenges Facing Universities: Quality. Leadership and the Management of Change.* Dunedin: University of Otago.

Meek, L. V. and Wood, F. Q. (1997) *Higher Education Governance and Management. An Australian Study.* DEETYA Evaluations and Investigations Program, Higher Education Division. Canberra: Australian Government Publishing Service.

Morgan, C. and Murgatroyd, S. (1994) *Total Quality Management in the Public Sector. An International Perspective.* Buckingham: Open University Press.

Moses, I. (1993) *Teaching Quality and Quality Earning in Professional Courses.* Canberra: Australian Government Publishing Service.

Mullins, G. P. and Cannon, R. A. (1992) *Judging the Quality of Teaching.* DEET Report, Evaluation and Investigations Program. Canberra: Australian Government Publishing Service.

National Board of Employment Education and Training (1997) *International Perspectives on Selection Methods of Entry into Higher Education.* Commissioned report 57. Canberra: Australian Government Publishing Service.

National Board of Employment, Education and Training; Higher Education Council (1997) *Quality Implementation and Reporting in Australian Higher Education.* Canberra: Macmillan.

National Committee of Inquiry into Higher Education (1997) *Higher Education in the Learning Society* (The Dearing Report). London: NCIHE.

Normann, R. (1984) *Service Management: Strategy and Leadership in Service Businesses.* New York: John Wiley & Sons.

Osborne, D. and Gaebler, T. (1992) *Reinventing Government: How the Entrepreneurial Spirit Is Transforming the Public Sector.* Reading, MA: Addison-Wesley.

Partlett, M. and Dearden, G. (1977) *Introduction to Illuminative Evaluation: Studies in Higher Education*. Santee, CA: Perfector Web Printing.

Peach, R. W. (1992) *ISO 9000 Handbook*. Arlington, VA: CEEM.

Peters, T. and Waterman, R. Jr (1982) *In Search of Excellence*. New York: Harper and Row.

Pollitt, C. (1990) *Managerialism and the Public Services: the Anglo-American Experience*. Oxford: Basil Blackwell.

Rosenbloom, D., Goldman, D. and Ingraham, P. (eds) (1994) *Contemporary Public Administration*. New York: McGraw-Hill.

Rothery, B. (1993) *ISO 9000*, 2nd edn. Aldershot: Gower Press.

Senge, P. (1990) *The Fifth Discipline: the Art and Practice of the Learning Organisation*. Sydney: Random House.

Shewhart, W. A. (1931) *Economic Control of Quality of Manufactured Product*. New York: D. Van Nostrand.

Shimberg, B. (1982) *Occupational Licensing. A Public Perspective*. Princeton, NJ: Educational Testing Service.

Sims, S. J. and Sims, R. R. (eds) (1995) *TQM in Higher Education. Is It Working? Why or Why Not?* Westport, CT: Praeger Publishers.

Standards Australia/Standards New Zealand (1995) *Quality System Guidelines Part 5: Guide to AS/NZS ISO 9001 for Education and Training*. Homebush: Standards Australia.

Stewart, J. R., Mauch, P. and Straka, F. (1994) *The 90-day ISO Manual. The Basics*. Delray Beach, FL: St Lucie Press.

Stufflebeam, D. L. and Shinkfield, A. J. (1985) *Systematic Evaluation*. Boston: Kluwer-Nijhoff.

Taylor, F. W. (1911) *The Principles of Scientific Management*. New York: Harper and Brothers.

Vroeijenstijn, A. I. (1995) *Improvement and Accountability. Navigating between Scylla and Charybdis: Guide for External Quality Assurance in Higher Education*. Higher Education Policy Series 30. London: Jessica Kingsley Publishers.

Walker, J. W. (1992) *Human Resource Strategy*. New York: McGraw-Hill.

Warner, D. and Crossthwaite, E. (eds) (1996) *Human Resource Management in Higher Education*. Buckingham: Open University Press.

Warren Piper, D. (1993) *Quality Management in Universities*. Canberra: Australian Government Publishing Service.

West, R. (1997) *Learning for Life (The West Report)*. Canberra: Australian Government Publishing Service and http://www.deetva.gov.au.

Western Australian Department of Training (1995) *A Quality System for Vocational Education and Training in Western Australia*. Perth: TAFE, Technical Publications.

Wolf, R. (1979) *Evaluation in Education*. New York: Praeger.

Woodhouse, D. (1995) *Audit Manual: Handbook for Institutions and Members of Audit Panels*, 2nd edn. Wellington: New Zealand Universities Academic Audit Unit.

Young, K., Chambers, C. and Kells, H. (eds) (1983a) *Understanding Accreditation*. San Francisco: Jossey-Bass.

Young, K., Chambers, C., Kells, H. and Associates (eds) (1983b) *The Changing Scope of Accreditation*. San Francisco: Jossey-Bass.

Significant journals ◼

American Association for Higher Education Bulletin.
Assessment Update.
Australian Journal of Public Administration.
Canadian Journal of Higher Education.
Chronicle of Higher Education.
Educational Record.
GATE Newsletter.
Higher Education in Europe.
Higher Education Management.
International Journal of Quality Science.
Journal of the Australasian Association for Institutional Research.
Journal of Educational Measurement.
New Zealand Education Review.
Public Administration.
Public Administration Review.
Quality Assurance in Education.
Quality in Higher Education.
Quality Magazine.
Review of Educational Research.
Review of Higher Education.
Society for Research into Higher Education International News.
Teachers College Record.
Total Quality Management.
Transfer. VET Research and Practice.

Significant newspapers ◼

Australian Higher Education Supplement.
Campus Review.
Times Higher Education Review and Supplement.

Significant conference proceedings ◼

Proceedings of the Association (and Australasian Association) for Institutional Research Conferences.
Proceedings of the GATE Conferences.
Proceedings of International Conferences on Assessing Quality in Higher Education.
Proceedings of the Quality in Higher Education Conferences.

INDEX

accountability, 26–7, 35, 59, 156
accreditation, 22–7, 33, 41–2
  beliefs about, 24–5
  common elements in
    accreditation models, 39–41
  'graduateness', 35–7
  international, 4–7, 34
  linking standards and education,
    33–4
  outcomes in, 37–42
  problems for, 25–6
  professional, 6, 34, 35–6, 36–7
  reasons for conducting, 26
  see also standards
Albrecht, Karl, 11, 124, 126, 147,
    149–50, 152
  phases in service success, 127–9
analysis, information and, 105
Andrews, R. J., 117
annual reviews, 53, 92–3
attributes of graduates, 117–19
Australia, 35, 44–5, 138–9, 150
Australian Medical Council (AMC),
    38
Australian Quality Awards (AQA)
    criteria, 120, 136–7, 143–4
awareness of national and
    international issues, 118

Ballantine, C., 31
Barker, J., 17

Barton, N., 132
Barzelay, M., 147–8
benchmarking, 2, 98–100, 156
  benefits of, 100
  identifying performance gaps, 101
  steps in, 99–100
  tool or process?, 98–9
  typology, 99
  see also best practice
Berggren, R., 37
best practice, 2, 100–19, 156
  assessing attributes of graduates,
    117–19
  checklist for client service, 129–31
  checklist for postgraduate
    training, 113–15
  checklist for research, 111–13
  client focus, 108–9
  feedback on, 116
  guidelines for achieving, 102–11
  information and analysis, 105
  leadership, 102–3
  organizational performance,
    110–11
  people, 106–8
  principles, 100–2
  quality of process, product and
    service, 109–10
  strategy, policy and planning,
    103–5
  in teaching, 115–16

Bloom, B. S., 67–8
borderline group method, 28
Bulgaria, 48
Burton, N., 31
business processes, 156
   re-engineering, 72–3, 140–3

Canada, 46
Candy, P. C., 117
Carlzon, Jan, 124
casualties of quality improvement,
   71–3
cause and effect diagram, 66
Center for Quality Assurance in
   International Education, 5
certification, 37
chain reaction, 72, 135
change
   cultural, 71–3, 146–7
   process of creating, 154
checksheets, 66
Chernay, G., 23
Chidley, M., 30–1
China, 47
client focus, 19–20, 71–2, 120, 152
   best practice, 108–9
client relationship management, 108
client satisfaction, 109, 116
clients, 2, 3, 156–7
   diversity and service, 147–8, 152
   knowledge of needs and
      expectations, 108, 128
   see also customers; stakeholders
communication, 108, 128–9
community leadership, 103
comparability, 34
competency-based standards, 30–1
competitive benchmarking, 99
competitiveness, 119–20
consultation, 141
continuous improvement, 27, 94,
   157
contrapreneurship, 72
contrasting of groups method, 28–9
control: planning and, 79
control charts, 66
corporate planning, 80
cost-effectiveness, 120
costs of quality improvement, 71–3

Council for National Academic
   Awards (CNAA), 43
Council on Higher Education, 45–6
course reviews, 59–65
   procedures, 61
   structure, 61
   template, 62–5
credentialing, 37
criterion-referenced testing, 29
critical success factors, 142, 157
Cronbach, L., 69
Crosby, Philip B., 9, 10, 12–16
cross-functional team, 157
cultural change, 71–3, 146–7
Cunningham, Stuart, 150
customers, 3, 147, 157
   interaction with organization,
      125–6
   see also clients; stakeholders
cycle time, 157
cycle time reduction (CTR), 140–3,
   157–8

Davis, C., 31
Deming, W. Edwards, 8–9, 17–18,
   51–2, 72, 135
   cooperation better than
      competition, 97
   deadly diseases, 122
   14 points, 12–16, 122–3
   quality process model, 52
Deming Prize, 9, 17, 71, 143
Denhardt, R., 152–3
design, 109
Dinham, S., 26
Directory of Advanced Training
   Opportunities in ACP states, 47
diversity, 147–8, 151–2
   TQS model, 124–6
documentation, 138
Doherty, G. D., 133–4

economic growth, 6
education
   applicability of ISO 9000, 133–5
   ISO 9000 standards clauses, 132–3
   linking standards and, 33–4
   participation and expenditure, 6
   principles for quality, 18–20

effectiveness, 158
effectiveness indicators, 88, 92
  research, 96–7
efficiency, 158
efficiency indicators, 88, 91, 92
  research, 97
Ellingham, C., 31
employer satisfaction surveys,
  117–19
empowerment of employees, 129
epistemic orientation model, 31
equivalency, 34
European Accreditation of
  Certification (EAC), 131
European Free Trade Association
  (EFTA), 131–2
European Network of Quality
  Assurance Agencies in Higher
  Education, 48
European Quality Award (EQA),
  120, 143–4
European Union (EU), 47–8, 131–2
evaluation, 68–70
  historical overview, 68–9
  training and development, 87–8
  uses of, 70
Evans, L., 26
excellence, fostering of, 25
exceptional value, 129
executive leadership, 126–7

feedback
  from clients, 116
  from employers, 117–19
Feigenbaum, A. V., 9, 12–16
financial indicators, 91
fishbone diagram, 66
Fisher, Ronald A., 8
Fleischaker, K., 31
Florida Power and Light, 71
forecasting, 79
French, S., 113
functional benchmarking, 99
functional organizations, 77–8
futuristics, 150

Gaebler, T., 71, 153
General Agreement on Trade in
  Services (GATS), 7

generic benchmarking, 99
Glass, G., 29–30
Global Alliance for Transnational
  Education (GATE), 4–6, 34, 151
global market, 145, 150–1
global media networks, 150–1
goal attainment method, 68–9
'graduateness', 6, 35–7
graduates: assessing attributes of,
  117–19

Harvey, L., 49
health care, 35–6
Higher Education Council, 44–5
Higher Education Quality Council
  (HEQC), 43–4
histograms, 66
history of quality management, 8–18
  Deming, 12–16, 17–18
  origins of quality movement, 8–9
  quality approach, 11–17
  quality gurus' principles, 12–16
  quality as service, 10–11
  role of Japanese, 9
  US experience, 10
Hong Kong, 47
human capital development, 6
human relations management
  thinking, 152, 153–4
human resource management
  planning, 106
  see also personnel management;
    staff development; workforce
    planning

indicators, 27, 158
  performance see performance
    indicators
information, and analysis, 105
Ingraham, P., 148
Ingstrup, O., 148
innovation, 109
inputs, 158
  accreditation, 40–1
Institute for Learning and Teaching
  in Higher Education, proposed,
  150
internal benchmarking, 99
international accreditation, 4–7, 34

International Network for Quality Assurance Agencies in Higher Education, 42
International Organisation for Standardisation (IOS), 4–5, 131
international standards *see* ISO 9000 standards
international students, 6, 92
Internet, 150–1
Ishikawa, Kaoru, 9, 66
ISO 9000 standards, 3, 4, 7, 131–40, 158
  adopting the approach, 135–7
  applicability to post-secondary education, 133–5
  clauses for education, 132–3
  origins, 131–2
  relationships to other quality frameworks, 137–9

Japan, 9
Japanese Union of Scientists and Engineers (JUSE), 9
job specification, 81–3
Jones, G., 135
Juran, Joseph, 9, 12–16, 122, 123, 147

kaizen, 9, 158
Kemmis, S., 69
key performance indicators (KPIs), 158
Kisner, C., 30–1
knowledge-based society, 145
knowledge workers, 145–6
Kotter, J. P., 154

leadership, 93, 146–7
  best practice, 102–3
  role in service success, 126–7
Leal, Barry, 137
learning
  lifelong learning skills, 117–19
  transformation of learning paradigm, 49, 154–5
learning organization, 18, 85
Leathem, P., 38
Lewis, Richard, 6
licensure, 36–7
lifelong learning skills, 117–19

Livingstone, S., 28
Loesch, L., 37
Lundquist, Robert, 138

Malcolm Baldrige National Quality Award (MBNQA), 120, 143–4
management, 103
  changes in thinking, 152–5
managerialism, 153–4
Mayo, Elton, 152
McDonald, J. P., 114
Meade, P. H., 95, 117
measurable outcomes, 158
  see also outcomes
measurement, 67–8, 158
media networks, global, 150–1
minimal competence, 28, 29–30
mission, 3, 158
morale, 107
Morgan, C., 72
Murgatroyd, S., 72

National Commission on Accrediting, 42
National Committee of Regional Accrediting Agencies, 42
National Evaluation and Accreditation Agency, 48
neo-Taylorism, 153–4
Netherlands, 48
Nethery, J., 31
Neville, S., 113
New Zealand, 49
Norcini, J., 30
Nordic School of Services, 124

objectives, 67–8
  and standards, 31–2
office skills, 118
operational plan, 158
operational units: performance indicators, 92–4
organizational performance, 110–11
Osborne, D., 71, 153
outcomes, 111, 158
  in accreditation, 37–42
  focusing on, 95–7
  measurement of, 67–8
outputs, 158

Pareto analysis, 66, 158
Partlett, M., 69
Patten, J., 133
Peace Lenn, M., 133
people *see* staff/people
performance
  best practice for organizational,
    110–11
  enhancement, 97
performance indicators, 3, 88–94,
    105, 158
  key (KPIs), 158
  limitations on use of, 90–4
  purpose, 89
  quantitative and qualitative, 89–90
performance management, 86–8,
    106–7
performance standard, 158
personal disposition, 118
personnel management, 79–84
  components, 81–4
Peters, T., 12–16, 71, 153–4
Pew Health Professions
    Commission, 36
Piper, David Warren, 89
planning, 74–97
  best practice, 103–5
  checklist for staff development
    planning, 84–6
  and control, 79
  focusing on outcomes, 95–7
  process, 104–5
  quality planning, 159–60
  scenario planning, 76–7
  setting strategic directions, 74–8
  strategic quality planning, 160
  strategy setting, 78–88
  use of indicators, 88–94
  workforce planning, 78–9, 80
  see also programme and planning
    reviews
policies, 93, 129
  and planning, 103–5
Pollitt, C., 152–3
position descriptions (PDs), 81–3
postgraduate training, 113–15
practices, 4–7
  commitment to quality practices,
    93

principles, 4–7
  quality improvement, 51–3
  quality model with client focus,
    19–20
private sector management, 154
process improvement, 110, 159
process management, 110, 159
process re-engineering, 72–3, 140–3
processes, 3, 93, 159
  business processes, 156
  quality of, 109–10
  quality improvement, 53–65
products
  quality of, 109–10
  and services, 149–50
professional accreditation, 6, 34,
    35–6, 36–7
profound knowledge, 17–18
programme-level accreditation, 22,
    33
programme and planning reviews,
    53–9, 60, 137–8
  model for, 56–9
public sector, 10–11, 153

qualitative indicators, 89–90
quality, 4, 159
  changing paradigm, 146–51
  defining, 11
quality approach, 11–17, 20–1
quality assessment, 24–5, 159
quality assurance, 10, 159
  international overview, 42–9
  see also accreditation; standards
Quality Assurance Agency (QAA),
    44
quality audit, 159
  accreditation and, 22–7
quality awards criteria, 120, 136–7,
    143–4
quality circles, 9
quality control, 9
quality control inspection, 121–2
quality cycle, 53, 54
quality gurus
  criticism of, 147
  principles and philosophies,
    12–16
  see also under individual names

quality improvement, 51–73, 159
  costs and casualties, 71–3
  evaluation, 68–70
  measurement, 67–8
  principles, 51–3
  processes, 53–65
  tools, 66–7
quality management, 17, 159
  characteristics of effective, 53
  with client focus, 19–20
quality management models,
    121–44
  CTR, 140–3
  ISO 9000 standards, 131–40
  quality awards criteria, 143–4
  service success models, 124–31
  TQM, 121–3
quality management system, 52–3,
    120, 159
quality management tools, 66–7
quality planning, 159–60
  see also planning
quality standards, 160
  see also standards
quality system, 95, 96, 160
quality tools, 160
quantitative indicators, 89–90

Radford, G. S., 121
Rancourt, R., 31
recognition for foreign
    qualifications, 34
recruitment of graduates, 119
re-engineering, 72–3, 140–3
reference group method, 29
reform TQM, 148
Reitherman, R., 27
research
  best practice checklist, 111–13
  indicators, 95–7
  postgraduate training best
    practice checklist, 113–15
results, 111, 160
reviews
  annual, 53, 92–3
  course, 59–65
  programme and planning, 53–9,
    60, 137–8
Robinson, R., 69

SAS, 124
Saunders, Ian, 154
scattergrams, 66
scenario planning, 76–7
scientific management, 121, 122,
    152, 153–4
Scriven, M., 30, 69
selection of students, 18–19
self-assessment, 57
Senge, P., 85
senior executives, 102–3
service, 154
  best practice checklist for quality
    of, 109–10
  defining, 127
  limitations of service standards,
    71–2
  quality as, 10–11, 146–51
service strategies, 71–2, 128
service success models, 75, 124–31
  client service best practice
    checklist, 129–31
  five phases, 128–9
  role of the leader, 126–7
  total quality service model,
    124–6
Sharp, C. A., 69
Shewhart, Walter A., 8, 122
Shingo, Shigeo, 9
Shinkfield, A. J., 70
six-sigma, 160
skills, graduates', 117–19
soft skills, 119
South Africa, 45–6
specific skills, 118
staff development, 83–4, 94
  checklist for planning, 84–6
  see also personnel management;
    training and development;
    workforce planning
staff/people
  best practice, 106–8
  empowerment, 129
  involvement, 106
  service success models, 129
staff profile information, 92
Stake, R. E., 69, 70
stakeholders, 69, 75, 94, 160
  see also clients; customers

standards, 1, 19–20, 23, 27–34, 160
  caveats on setting, 29–30
  competency-based, 30–1
  how they are set, 28–9
  international *see* ISO 9000
    standards
  linking education and, 33–4
  objectives and, 31–2
  performance standards, 158
  quality standards, 160
  use of, 32–3
  see also accreditation
statistical process control (SPC), 8–9
Stiwenius, Olle, 127
strategic directions, 74–8
  framework for strategic initiatives,
    75
  key questions to ask, 76
  optimum structure, 77–8
  scenario planning, 76–7
strategic plan: reviewing, 57–8
strategic planning, 80
strategic quality planning, 160
strategy: best practice, 103–5
strategy setting, 78–88
  checklist for staff development
    planning, 84–6
  performance management, 86–8
  personnel management, 79–84
  workforce planning, 78–9, 80
Strong, James, 72
structure, optimum, 77–8
student services, 92
Stufflebeam, D., 41, 69, 70
subject-based curriculum, 31
Suchman, E., 69
suppliers, 110
Sweden, 48
Swiss, J., 148
systems, 129
  quality system, 95, 96, 160

Taguchi, Genichi, 9
talk-walk balance, 146
targets, 160
Taylor, Frederick, 121, 152
teaching: best practice, 115–16
teaching qualifications, 116

time management skills, 118
total quality management (TQM),
    27, 72, 121–3, 136–7, 148, 160
  reform TQM, 148
total quality service (TQS) model,
    124–6
training and development, 83–8,
    107, 128–9
  evaluation, 87–8
  planning, 84–6
  see also staff development
transformation of the learning
    paradigm, 49, 154–5
transnational education principles,
    5, 7
Tyler, R., 68–9

United Kingdom (UK), 43–4
United States (USA), 10, 23–4, 42–3
University of Southern Queensland
    (USQ), 136–7

validation
  as accreditation, 33
  of reviews, 58–9
value, 146, 150
  exceptional, 129
value creation strategies, 152
values, 160
  integration of organizational,
    104
vertical structure, 77–8
vision, 160

walk-talk balance, 146
Waterman, R., 71, 153–4
Webster, W., 41
well-being, 107
Wolf, R., 69
work-related skills, graduates',
    117–19
workforce planning, 78–9, 80
workload indicators, 88
writing skills, 118

Zemke, R., 127
zero defects, 9
Zieky, M., 28